Creatively Lean

Creatively Lean

*How to Get Out of Your Own Way
and Drive Innovation Throughout
Your Organization*

Bella Englebach

Routledge
Taylor & Francis Group

A PRODUCTIVITY PRESS BOOK

First edition published in 2020
by Routledge/Productivity Press
52 Vanderbilt Avenue, 11th Floor New York, NY 10017

2 Park Square, Milton Park, Abingdon, Oxon OX14 4RN, UK
© 2020 by Bella Englebach

Routledge/Productivity Press is an imprint of Taylor & Francis Group, an Informa business

No claim to original U.S. Government works

Printed on acid-free paper

International Standard Book Number-13: 978-0-367-26210-5 (Paperback)
International Standard Book Number-13: 978-0-429-29656-7 (eBook)
International Standard Book Number-13: 978-0-367-27551-8 (Hardback)

Library of Congress Cataloging-in-Publication Data
Names: Englebach, Bella (Isabella), author.
Title: Creatively lean : how to get out of your own way and drive innovation throughout your organization / Bella Englebach.
Description: New York, NY : Routledge, 2020. | Includes bibliographical references and index.
Identifiers: LCCN 2019043227 (print) | LCCN 2019043228 (ebook) | ISBN 9780367262105 (paperback) | ISBN 9780367275518 (hardback) | ISBN 9780429296567 (ebook)
Subjects: LCSH: Creative ability in business. | Creative thinking. | Problem solving. | New products.
Classification: LCC HD53 .E5438 2020 (print) | LCC HD53 (ebook) | DDC 658.4/063–dc23
LC record available at https://lccn.loc.gov/2019043227
LC ebook record available at https://lccn.loc.gov/2019043228

**Visit the Taylor & Francis Web site at
www.taylorandfrancis.com**

For Sonja and Jensen.
May you always be as creative as you are today.

Contents

List of Figures

Preface

It is a couple of days before Christmas, and I am 11 years old. I have been waiting all day to FINALLY be alone in the house, and now my mother has left on an errand. None of my siblings are home, and my dad is still at work. I am about to commit a crime.

I start in the basement. The house is old; the basement, creepy. I'm not deterred from my mission by the atmosphere or the cobwebs, but my search here is fruitless, and I move to the ground floor. I check the pantry, and the back of the coat closet, and look under the stereo. Nothing. It must be upstairs. My heart is pounding as I check to see if the door to my parents' bedroom is locked. It isn't, and I enter, cautiously. The closet door is a little ajar, and I carefully widen the opening. On the floor I see shoes and, in the back, a large bag. Could this be it? Knowing that the crime I am about to commit is major is not enough to stop me. I look in the bag. Yes! There it is! A Junior Scientist Kit, complete with a real microscope! My joy is complete! With my Junior Scientist Kit, I could do experiments like a scientist, which would help me on my way to becoming a doctor!

When I was 11, my career goal was to be a doctor, but by the time I went to college, it was science itself that really attracted me. I studied biology and worked in labs. Learning something new by following the scientific method, doing experiments and interpreting experimental results were always exciting. But like many scientists, through the twists and turns of career, I left the lab and moved into the business end of research and development. "Business" was dramatically different from "science," or so it seemed. We didn't experiment anymore. We came up with solutions and implemented them. We were using Six Sigma, and in order to move quickly from "Analyze" to "Improve," often tried to implement the first solution that came to mind – usually with little effect.

In R&D we needed "innovation," and so I began to work with people who taught me a completely new way of thinking – Creative Problem Solving (CPS). CPS is a methodology to spur creative thinking and was invented by Alex Osborne, the inventor of brainstorming. (Learn more about CPS in Appendix 1.) CPS was remarkably effective in the research and development environment, and I eventually became a CPS facilitator.

Shortly afterwards, I started to learn about lean, and I quickly reignited the passion I had as a youngster for the scientific method, now encapsulated as the Plan-Do-Check-Act (PDCA) cycle. Lean and especially Lean Product Development (LPD) fit well in R&D, even though the business side still struggled to stop implementing solutions and start doing experiments.

What was I to do with CPS then? I felt a little like I had converted to a new religion. Could I still practice at least some of the old religion? The more I learned about lean, the more opportunities I saw to integrate CPS tools into lean thinking. I learned that the lean start-up and design thinking communities used some of these approaches, but no one seemed to leverage the full power of CPS with lean thinking, and most of my "lean colleagues" had no knowledge of CPS. Even the Lean Product Development community was at a loss to explain where ideas might come from, or how best to prepare other people to accept new ideas.

Perhaps this was all part of the "secret sauce" of lean at Toyota, that we tool-focused practitioners couldn't understand.

Worse yet, my CPS colleagues thought lean was an anti-innovative quality management system, so my conversations with them often slipped into me redefining and defending lean, and we struggled to learn from each other.

We often believe that:

- Deeply understanding the problem, through diligent definition, measurement, and analysis, will magically suggest the right solutions or countermeasures.
- "Creativity" is only about coming up with ideas for solutions and is not needed when we're trying to understand a problem.
- We can import solutions or countermeasures from other organizations (best practices) and they will work for us.
- Only certain people are "creative" or "innovative."
- We can survive if we only make incremental improvements, because breakthrough improvement will eventually arise from the accumulation of the incremental improvements.

These are all myths.

Back when I first started working on continuous improvement, a common lunchtime debate was whether what we called "process excellence" could exist in the same space as innovation. In our understanding of process excellence, the goal was standardization – once the standard was achieved, any innovation would create unnecessary disruption, and was to be avoided! Of course, most practitioners today would find such assertions ludicrous. Yet at the same time, we avidly study Toyota and other "lean" companies to grasp the key to process perfection, perfect flow, immaculate production, the kind of excellent product development that results in never missing a new product launch and almost always delights customers. We implement Kanban, kaizen, A3s (see Appendix 5), and 5S (or is it 6?), and wonder why our efforts fail to sustain, and why our incremental improvements rarely add up to transformative change.

There is a story, most likely apocryphal, of the tour group of business leaders who visited a Toyota plant, and saw a method of bringing parts to the operators. On arriving home, they rapidly implemented that method in their own plants, with varying levels of success. When they took a follow-up tour a year later, they were astonished to see that Toyota no longer used that method. Constantly innovating, the Toyota operators had now rethought the problem of getting parts and were using an entirely different solution. How the story ends depends on how good the business leaders were at understanding what had happened. In one version, they go home, and start to implement the new delivery method. In another, they go home and teach their operators to solve their own problems and create the innovations they need in their business.

Few of us can really SEE what is happening in an innovative environment like a Toyota plant. We're not there long enough when we visit. Like tourists, we take pictures of the artifacts, without understanding the culture.

The ability to develop an idea that is completely out of sync with popular understanding and make it into a business advantage has been part of the Toyota DNA since Sakichi Toyoda invented the circular loom in 1906. Over the years, Toyota has built a strong culture for innovation, based on the "Toyoda Precepts," which emphasize contributing to the Company *and* the overall good, striving to stay ahead of the times, and even "building a homelike atmosphere at work that is warm and friendly." Such a long history of innovation culture cannot be immediately or even quickly replicated in an organization with a culture that has not supported innovation. So then, it is a convenience for us to look to the artifacts of a lean company like Toyota.

We may easily implement those artifacts, believing that we're becoming "lean" and "innovative." (Of course, Toyota is not the only innovative company in the world, and may not be the most innovative, but Toyota's resilience and consistent business success, despite a multitude of obstacles, are one of the reasons we lean thinkers still look to Toyota City for the secrets of success.)

If we cannot replicate over a hundred years of an innovative culture, can we learn the skills of creativity in another way? The answer is yes, and that answer is found in creative problem solving.

This book brings the power of lean thinking and CPS together, so that you can practice the scientific method in business *and* develop and implement truly creative countermeasures to your business problems. It is written for the lean community, but if you're a CPS practitioner, and are working with a "lean company," this book will help you understand how to help your lean colleagues benefit from CPS without abandoning all the good things about lean.

(By the way, when my family met my future husband, they warned him that I had a bad habit of looking for my presents. I wonder how they knew?)

Acknowledgments

Deepest thanks to everyone who ever said to me, "When are you going to write a book?" Hope you like it!

Thanks to Michael Sinocchi of Productivity Press, who heard me speak and said: "That might make a good book."

Thanks to my husband, Rich Englebach, who provided cups of tea, and reminders that there is more to life than the laptop.

Thanks to Milo and Logan for their companionship during hours of writing and revision, and who are always ready to go for a walk when the writer needs to stretch her legs.

Thanks to Robin Keen, Jun Sutherland, Naomi Clark-Turner, and Erica Deuso, who provided feedback on the drafts.

Thanks to Jim Luckman, who was my first lean advisor, and who first asked me, "What problem are you trying to solve?" And thanks also to many lean-thinking friends and colleagues including Jackie Alligood, Terry Barnhart, Carol Ciletti, Alan Maloney, Maurice Prendergast, Katherine Radeka, Suzanne van Egmond, Jim Weber, Susan Wendel, and others too numerous to include, who inspire me every day on this journey.

Thanks to my talented son-in-law, Samuel Richman, who used his creativity to develop the illustrations for this book.

And most especially, thanks to Doug Reid, who has more than a little of Carlo in him. Doug, your encouragement, questions, and your skill for clarifying my mumbo-jumbo are deeply appreciated.

About the Author

Bella Englebach has been applying continuous improvement and lean thinking to operations and R&D for over 15 years. Trained as a scientist, she helps people see that the heart of improvement is the scientific method. Humans naturally respond to the scientific method, because as children we were all excited to ask why – and we all loved to conduct experiments to find out why! Along the way, many of us left that type of exploration behind, and came to believe that we were not good at problem solving or creativity.

Bella believes that everyone can regain their excited inner scientist to drive people-centered improvement for any type of organization. She works with leaders and managers to create environments where problems can be seen, innovative solutions can be discovered and tested, and people can truly drive improvement.

Bella spent 18 years at Johnson & Johnson, where she was a process excellence and business improvement leader, bringing the worlds of lean and creativity together in research and development, regulatory affairs, and IT implementations. She opened her own business, Lean for Humans, Inc, in 2018.

Bella is a Creative Problem Solving (CPS) Facilitator and is also an Associate Partner at New & Improved, Inc, a consulting firm specializing in helping organizations create the environments for innovation through the CPS approach. She is an experienced facilitator trained in continuous improvement, Creative Problem Solving, lean improvement, lean product and process development, and change management.

Bella was a member of the Board of Directors of the Lean Product and Process Development Exchange for six years, where she served as Board Secretary and Conference Chair. LPPDE is a nonprofit organization created to foster opportunities to grow and share the knowledge, expertise, and experiences that help organizations use lean product development to dramatically improve product development performance.

She is a popular speaker and workshop facilitator at lean, operational excellence, and continuous improvement conferences.

Introduction

One day a few years ago, my husband suggested that we take a cruise. Since I love to travel, you would think I immediately said, "Yes! I love that idea! Which cruise do you want to take?" But what I said was, "No."

Sometimes I don't even know why I resist a change. I know I have said "no" to many good ideas, without even thinking about why I'm saying no. If you asked me afterwards, I tell you "my gut" made that decision. Immediately afterwards, I would give perfectly logical-sounding reasons why my gut reacted in that way. In the case of the cruise, I immediately came up with quite a few objections to the idea (none based on any real facts or data). It would be too expensive, I said. We would be the youngest people on the ship. Our ability to really see the cities we were visiting would be extremely limited, and so on. I, the person who loves to travel, was obstructing my husband's idea before I had really listened or explored it.

For every change are instigators – and there are obstructers.

Creativity is intrinsic to humanity – and so is resistance. Just as we're made to be ideators, innovators, and change-makers, we're also made to resist creativity, distrust innovation, and obstruct change. *Resistance, distrust, fear, caution*: feelings seated in the "primitive" parts of our brains have kept us alive in times of famine, danger, and disaster. We're not always wrong when we fear newness or when we obstruct change. The question is whether we're making those judgments with our primitive brain or whether we're engaging the "human" parts of our brain. (And don't get me wrong. If your "fight or flight" reaction is engaged by the sight of a poisonous snake in your path, listen to your gut!)

I want to be a leader who drives continuous improvement. Intellectually I understand that everyone (including me) can think creatively – and likewise, I must understand that everyone (including me) can obstruct creative thinking.

Why? Because:

■ the way I react when I hear an idea
■ the way I ask for ideas (or not)
■ the way I coach my employees/team members (or tell them what to do)

affects the ability of my colleagues and teams to think creatively. The behavior of leaders has an indelible impact on the culture of an organization. Our self-awareness is vital to advancing innovation.

Many years ago, when I was a manager in a large company, one of my employees, Patrick, came to me with an idea. He was very excited.

"Hey Bella," he said. "I've been talking with my buddy, Pete. We noticed that we have a lot of empty office space around the building. In fact, we've done some data collection and we found that at any given hour, on any given day, about 40 percent of the offices are empty. People are in meetings, or they are traveling to other sites, so they are just not using their offices. Therefore, Pete and I would like to propose that we move forward with a shared office space plan." He put a spreadsheet front of me. "We could save a lot of money if we do this."

When Patrick came to me with this idea, I had been well trained in the things you should say when your employee brings you an idea. Intellectually, I knew that just saying "no" was NOT what I should do. What did I say?

"Wow, Patrick, that is quite an idea! In fact, that is the worst idea I have ever heard!"

Yes, that is exactly what I said. Then I came up with several "logical" reasons why it was such a bad idea, and why it wouldn't work.

As you read this story, you might be agreeing with Patrick, thinking this was a good idea, or you might be agreeing with me, thinking it was a bad idea. The fact is, at the time, I didn't have enough information about the problem Patrick was trying to solve, and therefore couldn't decide whether it was an idea we should explore or put aside. But my brain had literally told my gut that this was a bad idea.

What happened?

The concept of shared office space threatened my internal image of what it meant to be a manager – as someone who had long aspired to have an office, of my own, with a door, I couldn't imagine having the respect a manager "deserves" without an office and a door. The "threat" of losing MY office (as shallow as it might seem) elicited memories and associations of being made to feel "less." And that triggered the "fight or flight" reaction.

These uncomfortable memories and associations are stored in a tiny part of my brain: the amygdala. The amygdala is a key part of our "fight or flight" response and hangs on to bad experiences in order to keep us alive. My amygdala did its job, releasing stress hormones that quickened my heart rate and slowed my digestive processes (that is the "gut" feeling). I was reacting as if there was a poisonous snake in my path. There was no way, in that state, that I could listen to Patrick's idea, clarify the problem he was trying to solve, or evaluate whether to move forward with the idea. See Figure I.1 for a picture of what was happening in my brain. Because my amygdala was so busy defending against Patrick's idea, my frontal lobes didn't have a chance to weigh in.

What was Patrick experiencing? Happy and excited to share his idea with me, he was now faced with the poisonous snake of my reaction. Deep in his brain, his amygdala recorded this moment as a potentially dangerous situation. Perhaps his amygdala cataloged it with other bad reactions from other managers. In order to protect Patrick, his amygdala was preparing to save him from bringing ideas to managers in the future (and especially to me).

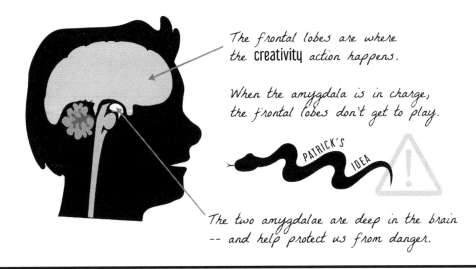

The frontal lobes are where the **creativity** action happens.

When the amygdala is in charge, the frontal lobes don't get to play.

The two amygdalae are deep in the brain -- and help protect us from danger.

Figure I.1 The "Fight or Flight Reaction."

Our brains were working exactly as they were designed to work. My brain was protecting me from the "threat" of losing my hard-earned office. Patrick's brain was learning of a new threat, from which it would protect him in the future. How many ideas would he bring me now? And what story would he tell his colleagues about what it was like to bring Bella an idea?

Moreover, my "logical" reasons that the idea was bad put Patrick on the defensive. If he wasn't in fight or flight mode already, he certainly was by the time he had reacted to each of my objections. And I never voiced my real objection: that my self-worth as a manager was at least partially based on having my own office – with a door. In retrospect, hearing and addressing that concern would have been key to managing the change, not only with me, but with other managers who treasured their hard-earned offices.

I learned that Creative Problem Solving has tools to save us from behaving as if ideas are poisonous snakes. The important thing about these tools is that I must practice using them. Just knowing about them is not enough to overcome the well-trained responses of my amygdala (which has done a great job of keeping me alive so far!)

Oh, my husband did manage to overcome my resistance to cruising, which was I think, really based on my fear of not being in control of the itinerary every day, as I was used to. It was an amazing vacation! It is funny though, when I tell people about it, how many of them say, "Oh, I wouldn't want to do that." Is that their amygdala talking?

But what about my own ideas? The converse of treating other people's ideas like poisonous snakes is that I can overvalue my own ideas. Once I have come up with an idea, I will defend it strenuously. Sometimes, the

Figure I.2   Patrick's Brain Learns of a New Threat.

idea deserves that strenuous defense. Often, it does not. But the same "gut" reaction that causes me to try to kill someone else's idea will cause me to try to kill their unreasonable (and reasonable) objections to mine. I will protect my idea, and my brain and gut will help me out. If I find myself becoming defensive (literally), this means that I'm not thinking with my frontal lobes.

None of the products of human ingenuity that we value today are the result of a single person's ideas. The best innovation is the result of combining ideas, of building ideas on other ideas, of breaking ideas and re-forming them. Creative thinking can be performed individually, but it is at its best as a team sport. As a leader, I can demonstrate what can happen when I allow my ideas to prodded, poked, broken, added to other ideas, improved, strengthened, or just used as inspiration for someone's even better idea.

In this book you will meet a manager who is learning both lean thinking and the tools of creative problem-solving. As you read each chapter, reflect on your own learning journey. Where are you getting in your own way as you seek to be innovative? How might you be both lean and creative? How might you lead others to be lean and creative?

Definitions

This book uses many words that have many meanings, depending on who is using them. Here are some key words:

A3 In the A3 methodology, the story of the resolution of a problem is captured on a piece of A3 or ledger-size paper. See Appendix 5.

Continuous Improvement Engagement of all members of an organization in increasing the effectiveness of the organization in meeting organizational goals.

Convergent thinking A thinking style for judging and selecting options and making decisions. Convergent thinking can be learned and developed.

Countermeasures Temporary responses to specific problems that will serve until a better approach is found or conditions change (Steven Spear).

Creative Problem Solving A process for solving the kind of problem that doesn't have a known answer, originally described by Alex Osborne and Sidney Parnes. Learn more in Appendix 1.

Creative Thinking A thinking style that permits people to view and solve problems from unusual or unorthodox perspectives. The two phases of creative thinking are divergent thinking and convergent thinking. Creative thinking can be learned and developed.

Creativity Novelty that is useful (Stan Gryskiewicz).

Divergent thinking A thinking style for generating many options. Divergent thinking can be learned and developed.

Gemba A Japanese word meaning the actual place where work is done.

Improvement kata A thinking pattern for problem solving based on the Toyota approach to management. See Chapter 14.

Innovation New ideas and inventions that create value.

Kaizen workshop an event, usually involving people from several functions, to create and put into practice significant positive revisions to a process/

Lean A socio-technical system for developing and managing people in organizations so that they can solve problems and continuously improve the organization *to deliver value to customers*, modeled on Toyota (and other organizations that have pursued "lean"). Practicing lean results in reduction of waste and increased customer satisfaction.

Lean thinking The thinking style of people who have been developed in a lean organization to see and solve organizational problems. Lean thinking can be learned and developed.

Problem A situation or state in which the desired performance is not being achieved.

Solution The responses or actions taken to bring performance to the desired level. A problem may need a set of solutions.

Chapter 1

A Meeting in the Parking Lot: Lean and Creative Problem Solving

Carlo pulled into the parking lot of Global Plumbing Supply just before the rain started. The weather forecaster on the radio had waxed eloquently about the incoming line of storms, and Carlo had made a mental note – and several physical notes – to remember an umbrella. But now, as he glanced around the front and back seats of his car, it was clear that the umbrella hadn't left the house with him that morning. This was no light spring shower, and there were at least 50 yards between his parking spot and the building entrance. Carlo checked his phone. He had 10 minutes before his meeting started, but there was no indication that rain was going to lighten up.

Carlo was about to make a dash to the door when a grey Toyota pulled into the space next to his car. Looking over, he saw his friend and coaching colleague, Linda. He knew that this engagement at Global Plumbing Supply was an unusual one, and that he would be sharing coaching responsibilities with another coach, but he hadn't realized it might be Linda. "All right," he said to himself, "this is a great development!" He was even more delighted when he saw that Linda was getting out of the car carrying a large umbrella. "Hey, Linda!" he greeted her.

"Carlo, nice to see you!" she replied. "Want to share my umbrella?"

Inside the lobby of Global Plumbing Supply, they introduced themselves to the receptionist. "I see you both are expected by Brandon Go, the CEO," replied the receptionist. "Mr. Go called and said he was delayed for 30 minutes or so. He sent his apologies and asked if you could wait for him. Please make yourselves comfortable here in the lobby."

Carlo and Linda chose a couch in the small waiting area. "This looks like a great time to catch up," said Carlo, taking off his jacket, "and to talk about this project."

"How did you get involved in this?" asked Linda.

"I got a call from a friend of mine who told me that this company was looking to improve their ability to innovate, and that she had recommended me as creativity coach for their executive team. I have to say I was surprised to get the call, as I had heard that Global Plumbing Supply had been starting a lean deployment, and as much as I admire the kind of stuff you do, I have never had a company that is deploying lean also ask about creativity."

Linda chuckled. "That might be the case, but maybe we can change things with this project. I was the one who suggested to Brandon that we build creative thinking into this lean deployment because I'm finding that my clients struggle with the kind of deep thinking that lean requires."
She handed Carlo an envelope. "Here is a briefing about GPS, and some background about the lean deployment. Look at it later. I'm glad you're on board. It is going to be fun to work together at last!"

"I never thought when we took that class together that we might work together some day," said Carlo. "I mean, lean thinking and creative thinking are really almost polar opposites."

Linda raised an eyebrow. "Carlo, how much do you know about lean thinking?"

"To be completely honest, not a lot. I know it is about quality control and manufacturing, standardization, things like that. Important, but not necessarily creative."

Linda raised the other eyebrow.

Carlo caught her look. "But since we seem to have some time on our hands, and since we're going to be working with each other, I think I need to learn more."

"As I do about creative thinking," replied Linda. "Although I know enough to recommend you join this project!"

"I'm ready to listen," said Carlo, "if you're ready for my questions. Pretend I don't know anything (which wouldn't be too far off). What is lean thinking?"

"Thanks for asking," Linda replied. "Everyone who is involved in lean in some way has their own preferred definition and visual model. You can think of this as Linda's definition of lean and lean thinking. I define lean as *a socio-technical system for developing and managing people in organizations so that they can solve problems and continuously improve the organization to deliver value to customers.* Lean is modeled on the business practices of Toyota and other organizations that have pursued 'lean.' Practicing lean results in reduction of waste and increased customer satisfaction."

"Hold on a moment," said Carlo, who was taking notes. "I know something about socio-technical systems, but how are you defining that?"

"Good question," Linda replied. "I tell people this: 'Socio-technical' means that lean involves people and their interactions, as well as technical tools. How people work with each other, coach each other, listen to each other, respect each other, and especially develop each other is critical to lean. And …" Linda paused, reflecting on something.

"And?"

"And the funny thing is, we're often taught the technical side of lean long before the people side is elucidated. In my lean training, the first this I was taught was 5S, a tool for workplace organization. It was only later in my career that I realized the real purpose of the tool was to give managers the opportunity to develop their employees to be able to solve problems that interfered with having materials always ready. I totally missed the point for about five years."

"Why do you think that was?" asked Carlo.

"I'm not completely sure, although I believe it is partly because people (and that includes me) like to have easy answers, and don't always want to think too deeply. Or we've been conditioned to think that we're not expected to think deeply at work – we should focus on getting work done. But I came to realize that what I was studying and practicing and eventually teaching wasn't just 'lean'." Linda made air quotes as she said "lean." "What it really was, was 'lean thinking.' "

"Which is?"

"Lean thinking is the thinking style of people who have been developed in a lean organization to see and solve organizational problems *to deliver value to customers.* Lean thinking can be learned and developed. And then I came to this realization: that the purpose of a lean system, is not to 'reduce waste' or 'improve flow of value to the customer.' "

"It's not?" asked Carlo.

THE PURPOSE OF THE LEAN SYSTEM *is to develop people who can reduce waste and improve the flow of value to the customer.*

Figure 1.1   The Purpose of the Lean System.

"Not at all. *The purpose of the lean system is to develop people* who can reduce waste and improve the flow of value to the customer."

"And then I realized, it doesn't matter what business someone is in. Whether someone develops software, works in a bank, makes automobiles, teaches high school students," Linda looked around the lobby, "even if they run a plumbing supply company. They can use lean tools to improve their organization. But they won't do anything sustainable until they start to develop people to be lean thinkers."

"And who are lean thinkers?"

"Lean thinkers are people who can see and solve problems. They may be good at using lean tools, or they may never use a 'lean tool.' What they excel at is using the scientific method to make observations about problems that need to be solved, create hypotheses on the root causes and solutions, test the solutions, and implement them."

"You know," said Carlo, "this is fascinating to me. My work is all about solving problems, especially problems that require innovative solutions. I can see now why you wanted to include creative thinking in this work. But I use a very specific problem-solving methodology, which I suspect is not the same one used in lean thinking. Tell me about how you solve problems as a lean thinker."

"The lean problem-solving process is basically the scientific method: make an observation, create a hypothesis, do some experiments to test the hypothesis, and update the hypothesis based on the results of the experiments. We capture this process as 'Plan-Do-Check-Act.'"

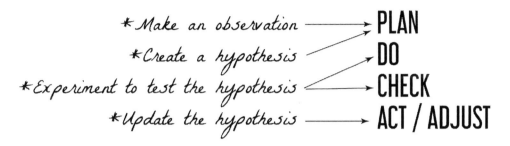

Figure 1.2   The Scientific Method and PDCA.

Carlo snapped his fingers and leaned forward. The receptionist looked over to see what was going on. "Oh sorry," Carlo said to the receptionist. "I got a little over-excited here." He turned back to Linda. "PDCA, isn't that the Deming cycle? I have heard of that."

"That's right," Linda replied. "Except W. Edwards Deming called it the Shewhart cycle. But what's important is that a lean thinker is always learning how to perform PDCA better. All the lean tools were developed and improved using PDCA."

The receptionist called out to them. "Mr. Go is ready to see you now. Do you need directions?"

"I know my way," said Linda. "Come on, Carlo, I think you're going to like Brandon."

They walked down a hallway and into an office area. A man in his mid-thirties was walking toward them with his hand outstretched. "Linda, great to see you. So sorry I had to keep you waiting. And this must be Carlo. I'm really looking forward to meeting you and learning about creative thinking. Linda speaks very highly of you!"

Brandon's office was not what Carlo expected for a CEO's office. They sat at a conference table; there was no desk. The office was small, and there were boxes of plumbing parts stacked in one corner.

Brandon spent a few minutes reviewing Global Plumbing Supply's history. He had inherited the company from his parents, just when he was about to start his MBA program. Since his parent's unexpected deaths, he had built the company from a regional to a national supplier, with significant increases in revenue. But as the company had grown, silos had developed, costs had increased, and while income continued to be strong, the operating margin had dropped precipitously. They had started to move the company from paper-based to digital processes, but that seemed to result in more rather than fewer problems. In the middle of this situation, Brandon had read a book about lean that he had picked up while delayed in an airport. "That was the best travel delay of my life!" he exclaimed. He had hired Linda's company to help GPS start their lean journey, and Linda had recommended that they bring Carlo into the project.

"So, Carlo, what is this Creative Problem Solving that Linda thinks can help us?"

Carlo was glad that he had forgotten his umbrella and that he and Linda had been able to chat in the lobby.

"As Linda was just reminding me, lean thinkers are getting better and better at seeing and solving problems. But what happens if the problem they need to solve requires new thinking? While lean was being developed at Toyota, Creative Problem Solving (CPS) was being developed in the US. CPS is a proven method for approaching a problem or challenge in an imaginative and innovative way."[1]

Carlo noticed that Brandon had a whiteboard in his office. "Do you mind if I write on your board?"

"No problem. Go ahead."

Carlo stood up and grabbed a marker.

"Like PDCA, the CPS approach has distinct steps for solving a problem and each of those steps uses divergent thinking and convergent thinking. Are you familiar with those terms?"

Brandon shook his head. "I mean, I could probably define them in general, but I want to hear it from you as they relate to creative problem solving."

Carlo wrote "Guidelines for Divergent Thinking" on the board. "Divergent thinking is the process of creating many options before evaluating them. For divergent thinking to flourish, CPS practitioners follow these guidelines:" He wrote, Defer Judgment, Combine and Build, Seek Wild Ideas, and Go for Quantity on the board under Guidelines for Divergent Thinking.

GUIDELINES FOR DIVERGENT THINKING

Defer Judgment
Combine and Build
Seek Wild Ideas
Go for Quantity

"I'll explain each one.

"*Defer Judgment* is waiting to decide if an idea or option is good, bad, or indifferent until a good list of ideas or options has been generated." Brandon nodded his head. "This helps with one of the problems we're having teaching PDCA to people. Everyone seems to get stuck at the first idea they have, and they either love it and try to implement it immediately or someone says, 'that won't work here,' and they give up. What's next?"

"*Combine and Build* – we realize that most great ideas are the combination or restructuring of other ideas, and we strive to combine ideas and build them together."

Brandon indicated the boxes of plumbing parts in the corner. "So true! Every one of those parts is evolved from other parts or the combination of parts. I can see how important that is. Tell me about seeking wild ideas."

"*Seek Wild Ideas* – Going beyond the usual ideas or options to come up with ideas that are not common, that give or use a new perspective. Being playful and sometimes even silly."

Brandon frowned. "Okay … that is harder to understand in a business context. Plumbing is not a silly business, despite all the jokes people make about plumbers."

Carlo nodded sympathetically. "It is hard to grasp when we think what we're doing is serious. But in situations where we need to solve a problem with no apparent solution, the wild idea might be the right idea. I'll give you an example from when the Wright Brothers were developing the airplane. They started out using boat propellers as prototypes. But the fluid dynamics of water are very different from air, and boat propellers didn't work. Then the Wright brothers had the idea to think of the propellers as rotary wings, that could create lift and thrust, rather than a push, as a boat propeller does. Crazy to think of putting more wings on a biplane that already had wings, right? But once they allowed themselves to think that wild idea, they were able to shape propellers that worked."

"Makes sense," said Brandon. "And the last rule for divergent thinking?"

"*Go for Quantity* – The first 5 or 10 or 20 ideas or options may not be innovative. Stretching the mind to generate dozens of options or ideas, even if it takes a little longer, will be beneficial."

Brandon looked at Linda. "That seems like an important thing to do when we have people getting stuck for ideas to solve problems. Does Creative Problem Solving have techniques to help people do this?"

Carlo smiled. "CPS has dozens of tools to help individuals and groups generate longer, better, more creative lists of options and ideas."

"So, then what do you do once have that long list of ideas? I can foresee us getting just as stuck deciding on which idea to move forward."

Carlo was happy to answer this. "Divergent thinking isn't enough. Simply generating lots of ideas or options won't help you solve a problem. Convergent thinking is required to evaluate ideas, narrow down your list, strengthen ideas, and make good decisions about what goes forward. Like divergent thinking, there are guidelines for convergent thinking. These were developed by Scott Isaksen and Don Treffinger and proposed in their book *Creative Problem Solving: The Basic Course* in 1982."[2]

Carlo wrote on the whiteboard: Be Deliberate; Check Your Objectives; Improve Your Ideas; Be Affirmative; Consider Novelty.

GUIDELINES FOR CONVERGENT THINKING

Be Deliberate
Check Your Objectives
Improve Your Ideas
Be Affirmative
Consider Novelty

"Allow me to explain.

"*Be Deliberate* – After spending a long time coming up with options, it is a temptation to choose options quickly and without a fair consideration of each. You should undertake this deliberately and allow enough time.

"*Check Your Objectives* – It is easy to lose sight of *why* you're solving a problem. Validate that the choices being made are ones that impact your objectives."

"That's what we do in our A3s, right, Linda?" queried Brandon.

"Exactly!" Linda responded.

Carlo continued. "*Improve Your Ideas* – Any idea or option may 'need work' before being ready to move forward. Don't discount the idea that isn't quite ready. Take time to improve it.

"*Be Affirmative* – Focus on what you want, not what you don't want. Stay positive to improve your thinking.

"*Consider Novelty* – If you're using CPS, it is most likely because you need innovation. Don't throw out the most unusual ideas rashly. Spend time with them to see their value, improve them, perhaps rework them."

"Yeah, I can understand that. It would do no good to come up with wild ideas if we throw them out immediately."

Carlo continued. "CPS also has dozens of tools to help the lean thinker practice effective convergent thinking. And each tool has a specific purpose, depending on your needs. Some tools help you strengthen ideas, others help you prioritize, and others help to evaluate or compare ideas."

Brandon stood up. "This is great. Linda, thanks so much for bringing Carlo in. I think adding CPS tools to our lean deployment is going to help us solve problems better. I'm looking forward to learning how the two of you put this together for us."

"With you" said Linda. "Not for you."

"Right," said Brandon. "With us."

PRACTICE THIS TODAY

Observe yourself as you go through your day: what is your "gut" reaction to change and new ideas? Are you excited, or does your mind immediately jump to problems? Do you defend your ideas at the expense of other people's ideas? Why do you think you react the way you do? Can you really trust your gut?

Notes

1. www.creativeeducationfoundation.org/creative-problem-solving/.
2. Isaksen, Scott G., and Treffinger, Donald J., *Creative Problem Solving: The Basic Course* (New York: Bearly Ltd, 1985).

Chapter 2

One of Those Surprise Meetings

"Did you hear?" asked Georgia, in an ominous tone, as she pushed the button on the coffee machine. "We have a new corporate initiative." It was only 7:30 a.m., but it was clear that this was not Georgia's first cup of coffee. "Do you want to hear it from me, or do you want to wait until the staff meeting this afternoon?" As their Director's administrative assistant, Georgia was often the first to hear news, and the first to share it.

Beth suppressed a sigh. She wanted to get to her desk and get started so she could leave a little early to get to her son's soccer game. It was clear that Georgia was eager to share the news, and it might be better to get it out of the way.

"What staff meeting? I didn't see it on my calendar."

Georgia smirked. "That is because this is one of those 'surprise' meetings." She used air quotes with the word "surprise." "Roberta asked me to send it out first thing this morning." Georgia leaned into stage whisper. "We're going to start doing *lean*."

"What does that mean?" asked Beth.

Georgia's tone dropped even lower. "You know business hasn't been great recently. Lean usually means 'Less Employees Are Needed.' If I were you, I would brush up on my resumé."

Georgia spotted Edric, Beth's colleague, down the hall. "I'd better clue Edric in. See you this afternoon."

This had started out to be a good day. Beth's ex had dropped her son off in time for the 7:00 "early" school bus, and traffic had been light on the way to Global Plumbing Supply's Philadelphia headquarters. But now

Beth's mood was sinking. As assistant director for US operations, she knew enough about the numbers to realize Georgia was correct about the state of their business. She had only been in her role in Roberta's leadership team for a year, and if people were going to be let go, she really couldn't claim any seniority. But she had too much to do this morning to work on her resumé.

Back at her desk, she opened her email, and saw the staff meeting appointment for 2 p.m. Georgia had sent it on behalf of Roberta, the Director of Sales and Customer Fulfillment, and all of Roberta's direct reports were invited. It was only scheduled for 30 minutes, so there was still a chance that she could leave by 3:30 for the soccer game at 4 p.m. She pressed "accept" and then spent 10 minutes rescheduling a previous meeting.

As usual, her inbox was full of mail, even though she had cleared it while her son was doing homework the night before. Before she could get started, an instant message popped up on her screen.

Mo Khan: Hi boss. You got a moment?

Beth knew if Mo, the supervisor of the contact center was messaging her, it was probably important. She replied quickly.

beth brickell: For you, always! What's up?
Mo Khan: We have an issue in the contact center. Can I call you?
beth brickell: You bet. Call my mobile.

As soon as her phone rang, she answered it. "Good morning to you, Mo!"

Mo groaned. "Likewise. Listen, things are a little out of hand here this morning." Beth knew that their main customers, plumbers, started their days early, and by 7:30, many were already on the job, and calling about parts they needed. "You know that we have started to use a new online ordering system, right? Customers can use their phones to order parts, and that is supposed to reduce the number of calls to the contact center. Guess what?"

"What?"

"We're getting more calls. More calls, not less. The past week has been so bad that we have a backlog of calls – people who left messages who we have to call back. That means the contact center employees can't take calls. So, we're getting more of a backlog."

"And I'm guessing that the people you're calling back are not happy because their call went to voicemail."

Mo sighed. "You got it. But that's not all. This morning three of my folks called in sick. I don't know if it's the flu or stress, but that backlog is getting worse."

"Mo, what can I do to help?"

"Beth, I hate to ask this, but I'm going to need permission to hire some temps – maybe even some more permanent employees to get through this."

"We don't have budget for that."

"I'm afraid we're going to lose customers if we don't solve this problem. We need more people. At least until the bugs in the app are worked out."

Beth knew that she was going to have to talk to Roberta about this. She quickly checked Roberta's calendar to see if there was an open spot, but there was nothing available until 4:30 p.m., and that would mean she wouldn't be able to get to the soccer game.

"Mo, let me see what I can do. I don't have budget, but maybe Roberta does. I will send her an email, but she usually doesn't respond to email for a couple of days. But I will do everything I can to get you an answer today. Is there anything else I can do?"

"You wanna come answer some calls?"

"I wish I could, but I'm not trained for contact center anymore, and I have my own backlog." She could tell Mo was frustrated. "I'm really sorry. Tell the crew I have their backs."

Beth sent an instant message to Georgia to ask her to hold the 4:30 p.m. slot on Roberta's calendar for her, but Georgia didn't respond. Beth sent Roberta a calendar appointment, hoping either Roberta or Georgia would see it. She knew better than to instant message or call Roberta. Roberta was not, as she put it, "an IM person," and rarely answered her phone.

Beth turned her attention back to her own backlog of email. There were customer complaints that she had been copied in on, notifications of corporate required training that she was late on, calendar appointments that needed to be accepted, which meant she had to prioritize and reschedule existing appointments. Clearly, a lot of people had been working from home last night, sending emails, and setting up meetings.

"I know how the contact center folks feel," she thought to herself. "I need a sick day." A notification appeared on her screen telling her she had a meeting in five minutes. She had only been at work an hour, but she could tell it was going to be a long day.

Beth felt almost sick as she entered the conference room for the 2 p.m. meeting. Was it concerns about what she would hear in the meeting, or the sandwich she had snatched for lunch in between phone calls and meetings? All day, the rumor mill had been pumping out worrying stories. Beth had already heard from colleagues that all the permanent employees in her contact center were going to be replaced with contractors in another country, and that budgets for new projects were going to be slashed. Up to 25 percent of employees were going to be laid off, and to top it off, they were going to have to pay for their coffee and all training and non-sales travel were going to be eliminated. Beth had tried to avoid the rumors, but they had popped up in phone conversations, in instant messages, and in the restroom.

It seemed that others in the meeting shared her anxiety. The mood in the room was solemn, and people were avoiding eye contact with their colleagues.

At 2:03, Roberta swept into the room and took her place at the head of the conference table. She was smiling and relaxed, and warmly greeted her direct reports. Georgia sat in a chair in the corner, thumbing through her phone.

"Good afternoon, everyone. Thank you for making time for this meeting. Let me check that everyone is here."

Beth glanced around the room. All seven of Roberta's direct reports for US sales and customer fulfillment, including Georgia, were in their seats. To Beth's left was Bob O'Toole, the Southeast area sales manager. Bob had his laptop open, and Beth could see he was looking at LinkedIn. Next to Bob was Marisol Rivera, who was responsible for the Southwest. Marisol also had her laptop open. She was working on a spreadsheet and had at least five IM windows open. To Marisol's left, was Beth's closest work friend, Keisha Cobb, who managed the parts warehouse. Keisha reported to Beth and was invited to Roberta's staff meetings because the company considered her to be a high-potential employee. Rounding out the group was Edric Santos, the area manager for the Northeast and the Midwest, and Judy McEntire, the area manager for the Northwest. Judy and Edric, who had started at Global on the same day more than 20 years ago, were whispering to each other, but stopped when Roberta spoke.

"I'm so glad I could have this meeting on a day when you're all in the office," Roberta started. It was unusual that all the area managers were in. They each supervised a team of salespeople in their regions and were frequently "on the road."

"I have some exciting news to share. As you know, the Directors have been at an off-site meeting for the past week, and I'm looking forward to giving you some insight into a new direction we're taking as a result of that meeting." She glanced around the room. "Everyone, please close your laptops and phones – I want your full attention for this.

"Six months ago, as you're probably aware, the executive team performed a review of the business." Beth remembered when there had been consultants in the building. She had been interviewed and asked for metrics from her area. The consultants disappeared as quickly as they came, and Beth had not thought about them since.

Roberta continued. "The review identified areas of strength and areas that need to improve." Beth held her breath. The problems in the contact center were well known and had only gotten worse since the implementation of the online ordering system. Maybe the rumor about outsourcing the contact center was true.

Roberta handed out some papers that were stacked in front of her. "This will help you understand what was found in the review, and the areas for improvement. As I pass this out, it is important that we talk about confidentiality."

Beth knew what was coming next. As Roberta's direct reports, each with their own staff, there were topics and information that they were not to share with their staff. The information on these sheets of paper was something they would be told not to share.

"For the next couple of weeks, this information is company confidential – not to be shared outside the company. However, I expect you to share this with your staff in the next couple of days. I will meet with you before you meet with our staff and I would be happy to join your staff meeting if you need me to."

Beth looked at the paper. It was large, ledger-size, and had the name of the CEO, Brandon Go, on the top line. The title was "Improving Performance of Global Plumbing Supply."

Roberta was handing out a second sheet. This one had Roberta's name on it and was entitled "Improving Performance of Sales and Fulfillment." Unlike Brandon's document, this one had several blank sections.

"These." said Roberta, "are A3s." She smiled broadly. "They are tools to help us on our improvement journey. Let's take a look at Brandon's A3 first.

"As you can see, Brandon is setting out some ambitious goals for us. Much of the time at the off-site was reviewing and discussing these goals with him, so that each Director understands them, and buys into them, and sees how our departments can contribute.

"The five goals are:

1. No safety incidents.
2. Improve employee engagement by 50 percent.
3. Improve net promoter score to 80.
4. Bring five innovative new offerings to market.
5. Increase operating margin to 10 percent."

Beth put her hand up. "Roberta, I need to ask a question." Roberta nodded. "I'm sure you have lots of questions. I did when I saw this – or the first version of this that Brandon shared with us."

Beth paused for moment. She wanted to ask her question carefully, so she didn't betray her anxiety.

"These all look great, but doesn't achieving Number 5 mean that we can't achieve the others?"

Roberta leaned forward. "Tell me more about what you're thinking."

"Our operating margin is only around 3 percent now. Our biggest cost driver is salaries and benefits. So, to increase the net margin, we will have to let people go." Beth's mouth was suddenly very dry. "And if we let people go, that will mean the employee engagement for the remaining employees will sink. And turnover will go up among the remaining employees. And that will create customer service and safety issues. So, I'm not getting it." Glancing around the room, she noticed that her colleagues were avoiding looking at her.

"Thanks, Beth, for that question." Roberta chuckled. "I had the same question. When we're pushed on operating margin, we always cut costs, and usually at the expense of people. But Brandon believes that we can grow the top line and learn to manage the bottom line better. Some of that top line growth will come from new offerings, but we can also contribute with better sales and new services for our customers. Did you notice that these are three-year goals? We're not expected to do this all at once. But we do need to get started."

In the next 20 minutes, Roberta reviewed Brandon's A3 with her team, and listened carefully to their input. Beth watched Roberta with awe. This was seemingly a new Roberta. She was known as a brusque manager, quick with decisions and typically did not seek feedback.

"That must have been some off-site!" Beth thought to herself. "I wonder how long this will last."

As promised, the meeting ended by 2:30, and Roberta asked each person to work with Georgia to find time on her calendar for a one-on-one before their own staff meetings. Beth was the last to leave the room. She wanted to catch Roberta and let her know about the requested meeting to discuss the contact center staffing issues.

"We don't need to meet," said Roberta. "You know I don't have budget for more headcount. I would like you to go and spend the day in the contact center tomorrow and see what is really happening there."

Beth's heart sank. This was the old Roberta, quick with a decision, even if it wasn't well-thought-out.

"I have several important meetings tomorrow. It is not a good day for me."

Roberta looked Beth in the eyes. "There is nothing more important right now than you going to see what is really happening there. Cancel those other meetings. I have your back on that. And on Wednesday, meet me in my office at 10 a.m. I hired some coaching help for you, and you need to get acquainted. Oh, and Beth, how is Connor's soccer going?"

PRACTICE THIS TODAY

How does the rumor mill operate in your organization? What does this say about the level of interpersonal and interdepartmental trust? How does it impact people's ability to see and solve problems and be creative and innovative? If there are a lot of rumors and stories, what are the ways you can change the conversation?

Chapter 3

Carlo Meets the Management Team

Linda and Carlo were sitting in the cafeteria waiting for a meeting with Brandon and his management team. Again. Carlo didn't mind. He enjoyed having the time to sit and chat with Linda and learn more about lean and her way of thinking about an organization. He could see that Linda wasn't quite as happy as he was to be kept waiting, but he thought she was happy to learn from him as well.

"Linda," he said, "I think stories are incredibly important. Is there a story about lean that encapsulated the whole approach for you?"

"Wow, interesting question. Well, yes, there are several stories, but this is one of my favorites.

> A new Toyota employee was given a problem to solve. He eagerly started to work on the problem, and in a few days, came up with some countermeasures he wanted to try. He proudly showed his manager, expecting accolades.
>
> The manager grunted, 'Hmmph. No good. Go back. Think deeper.' "

Carlo nodded his head. "That is surprising. And it is also very, I don't know, Zen. I could imagine a character in a martial arts movie – or maybe Yoda saying that."

"Is it?" asked Linda. "Surprising? And I think Yoda would say, 'Think deeper, you must.' "

Carlo chuckled. "He would! It is surprising to me because I'm so used to encouraging people. And I think I would be surprised to hear an American manager say that. They might tell the employee what is wrong with their solutions, or what the right answer is. Both of which, incidentally, would impact the employee's desire and ability to bring new ideas forward."

"Exactly." Said Linda. "Exactly."

They saw Brandon waving to them. "I guess it's showtime," said Carlo, waving back.

Brandon's direct reports were packed into his office. Today was the day that Carlo was going to give them a briefing on creative thinking. Carlo stood near the whiteboard. He wasn't a fan of slide presentations and had decided to speak from the heart and used the whiteboard to illustrate his points.

He started with his usual opening. "I can't go for five minutes in a discussion on the need for innovation without someone telling the stories of the organizations that failed to recognize that their market was shifting and just didn't innovate when they had to. You know the stories: Kodak, Blockbuster, your local taxicab authority, your favorite bookstore, and the local coffee shop. We know that continuous improvement is required *just to stay in business*, and that it is better to be at the forefront of innovation rather than the organization playing catch-up. Does that make sense for your business?"

The leadership team nodded their heads. Carlo took that as license to continue.

"Unfortunately, even though these stories are well known, creative thinking is still not treated like a basic need or a basic skill even in lean organizations."

Brandon interrupted. "And we're not a lean organization – yet."

Carlo picked up a marker and drew on the whiteboard. "This is a common formula or process for improvement. Tell me what you think of it."

"You see a problem, you do some root cause analysis, which suggests a solution (I call this 'magic happens'), sometimes you test the solution, but often you don't, you implement the solution and it works."

No one appeared to have questions, so he went on. "It doesn't matter what improvement approach you employ; you can fall into the 'magic happens' trap. As you move through your problem-solving approach, there is a point at which you need to come up with potential solutions or, as Linda would say, 'countermeasures.'" He glanced around the room. Everyone was leaning forward, expectantly. He continued. "We believe that examining the problem, measuring it, determining the root causes will help us to find the solutions. And I've seen magic happen, so I can attest to the fact that magic does happen – sometimes. Sometimes analysis does suggest solutions

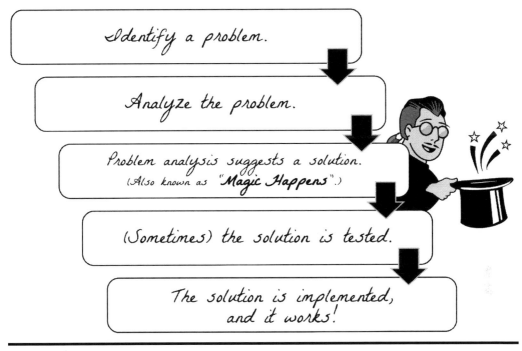

Figure 3.1   Magical Problem Solving.

and countermeasures to try, and if you're lucky, some of them work and are accepted. Or perhaps a good practice or tool from another company or department will be just the thing your organization can implement with success. You feel smart."

A woman raised her hand. "Yes, but …"

Carlo nodded at her.

"But most of the time, magic doesn't happen."

"And what might be the reasons for that?" asked Carlo. "And remind me of your name?"

"I'm Roberta, Director of Sales and Fulfillment. Perhaps you don't have good ways to measure the problem, and some problems don't have readily apparent solutions even after what seems like a well-conducted analysis."

Another director chimed in. "Linda has been teaching us a lot about the importance of finding the root cause, but sometimes you can't identify solutions that address the root causes. I know we are supposed to test our way to the right set of countermeasures, but it is not always clear even where to start. What to try first. And my team is getting frustrated."

Jeremy, the HR Director spoke up. "Well, sometimes the solution to the root cause is obvious."

Roberta nodded. "Or, Jeremy, we think it is obvious. But sometimes the 'obvious' solution is not one that that people can accept."

Jeremy made a scoffing sound. "I would think that for most of the problems in our business, there is a 'best practice' we can borrow. I don't know why we have to go and look to reinvent wheels all the time."

"Jeremy has a good point," said Linda. "That's why I'm teaching you and your employees a lot of lean thinking tools and concepts, because many of the problems that you have are not particularly unusual." A few people laughed, nodding their heads. Linda continued. "Yes, you know what I mean! But sometimes the best practice we had hoped to borrow fails in your environment."

Roberta had been listening intently. "We don't want to just catch up to our competition, we need to do better than them. So, we can't just borrow best practices all the time anyway. We are going to have to be more innovative in our solutions. We can't rely on waiting for magical thinking to get to those innovative solutions."

"That was great," said Carlo. "Lots of reasons why magic might not happen. And there is at least one more: Perhaps you just can't figure out what the real problem is that needs to be solved." He noticed that Linda was taking notes in the black notebook she carried everywhere with her.

"People and organizations who can't make the 'magic' happen, despite the strength of their tools for making problems visible and analyzing the problems, will fall behind those who understand how the magic really works. The magic starts to work when we understand how to leverage our intrinsic human ability for creative thinking."

> The magic starts to work when we leverage our human ability for creative thinking.

One of the attendees laughed. "You do know that this is a plumbing supply company, right, not an art studio?"

"I do," Carlo replied. "And I have great faith in the creativity of plumbers and the people who supply the parts they need. I know plumbers are creative, because every time I go to a new hotel it takes me at least five minutes to figure out how to turn the shower on. It's always different." Everyone chuckled. "But I have great faith in you, plumbing supply people, because everyone has some ability to be creative, and everyone can build their skills for creativity."

Linda raised her hand. "Carlo, do you mind if I weigh in here? I'd like to offer a perspective from the 'lean thinking' side."

"That would be great, Linda, thanks!"

Linda stood up. "When we think deeply as we define the problem, when we think deeply as we work out how to measure it, when we think deeply as we analyze our data, aren't we more likely to address the correct issues?"

Carlo saw heads nod around the table.

"When we think deeply as we come up with countermeasures and solutions, aren't we more likely to arrive at the best ones?"

Brandon answered this time. "We need the best solutions, so we do need to think better, more deeply."

Linda continued. "When we think deeply when we implement our changes, aren't we're more likely to be successful in making the change happen?"

Another executive spoke up. "We're not good at making and sustaining changes."

"Linda," said Carlo, "why don't you tell them the story you told me when we were sitting in the cafeteria?"

Linda smiled. "OK."

'A new Toyota employee was given a problem to solve. He eagerly started to work on the problem, and in a few days, came up with some countermeasures he wanted to try. He proudly showed his manager, expecting accolades.

The manager grunted, 'Hmmph. No good. Go back. Think deeper.'

Carlo saw that the meeting attendees looked puzzled. Linda kept going. "If the result of lean thinking is the reduction of waste, isn't it wasteful to address the wrong problem, and to attempt to implement solutions and countermeasures that have no chance to solve the real problem? How might we 'Go back and think deeper?' Why don't we think deeply? What's stopping us?"

There was silence in the room. Finally, Roberta spoke again.

"I have had some fantastic managers in my career. But I have never had a manager say to me, 'Hmmph, no good. Go back. Think deeper.'"

She looked at Brandon.

"I know I haven't ever said that to someone," Brandon mused. "I have told people what I thought they should do instead. More than once."

Carlo turned to Roberta. "Is that all that is stopping you from thinking deeply? Not having been asked to?"

Brandon raised his hand.

"We move very fast in this business. We don't have time to think deeply."

"Okay," said Carlo. "Do you have time to not think deeply? Can you afford not to implement innovative solutions?"

> Do you have time to NOT think deeply?

Everyone laughed.

"One of the main reasons that people don't think deeply is that they don't know how. The Creative Problem-Solving Process provides tools to use with your lean problem-solving approach to help you think deeper at every stage."

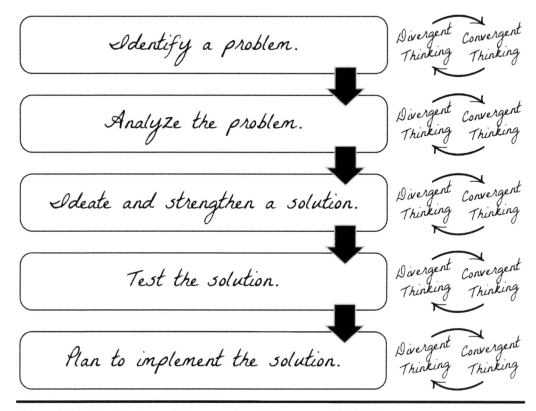

Figure 3.2 The Rhythm of Divergent and Convergent Thinking.

Carlo erased "magic happens" from the whiteboard, changed some of the wording in the boxes, and added "divergent thinking" and "convergent thinking" to each step of the process.

"Deep thinking means creative thinking. Thinking creatively means: Using DIVERGENT THINKING and CONVERGENT THINKING deliberately and separately."

> Thinking creatively means using divergent thinking and convergent thinking deliberately and separately.

"You'd better define that," said Linda.

"Divergent thinking means coming up with multiple options. Convergent thinking means deliberately choosing and strengthening options.

"This simple cycle of divergent and convergent thinking can be applied to every step of your favorite improvement process. This cycle separates the work of ideation from the work of judging ideas, allowing our brains to focus energy on generative work and selective work, giving each its own time in the process. We have plenty of ideas to work with, and we don't kill them before they have been properly reviewed and considered."

Carlo looked around the room. He was happy to see that he still had their full attention. "What questions do you have?" he asked.

Roberta raised her hand. "Can I talk to you about working with my section? I have a direct report in mind who I think would benefit from this as she starts to learn lean thinking. Her name is Beth Brickell."

PRACTICE THIS TODAY

What are the top "intractable problems" your organization or team are facing? Is your organization systematically addressing these problems using effective innovation approaches and tools? How might you change this?

Chapter 4

A Day in the Contact Center

The next day, Beth walked into the contact center at 7 a.m. She had given Mo a heads up that she would spend the day with him and his team. "You know, we're not going to pretty things up for you," he had said. "We're scrambling too much right now."

The contact center was a large open "bullpen." Monitors on the wall showed the number of calls coming in, calls being answered, calls on hold, and calls dropped or sent to voicemail. At 7 a.m., the plumbers on the East Coast were just getting to their first jobs, and calls were light. Each contact center employee had their own monitors and wore a headset. Even though they were in an open workspace, they did not look at each other while on a call.

Beth felt a little apprehensive. She had started in the contact center and had risen to day shift supervisor before being promoted to Roberta's team. She used to be very familiar with contact center operations, but it had been a long time since she had taken a call.

Mo met her at the door. "Hey, boss, what's cooking?"

Beth smiled. It was great to see Mo in person. These days, Beth's contact with him was usually limited to teleconferences and IM chats, even though they worked in adjoining buildings.

"You tell me." She glanced around the room. "Doesn't seem so crazy right now."

"Yeah, well, wait an hour. Then the customers will start to discover their missing orders and defective orders from yesterday, and we'll start getting calls from guys out on jobs who need to order SKUs from the warehouse."

Beth was puzzled. "I thought they were supposed to use the new online ordering system and not call in any more for orders."

"Some old dogs don't want to learn new tricks. Some of our customers don't have smartphones or tablets. And some do, and tried the new system, but don't like it too much. There are definitely problems with it."

Mo handed Beth a cup of coffee. "One cream, right? See, I remember!"

"Thanks, that's right. So, what do you want me to do? Like I said yesterday, I'm not trained on the new procedures, so I don't think it is a good idea for me to take calls."

"It means a lot to the crew that you stopped by here and are interested in our problems. But, to be honest, a couple of them were nervous about you being here. I told them that you're mostly harmless." Mo indicated an empty station. "I suggest you hang out here for a while, watch what is going on and, in a little bit, you can listen in to some calls."

Beth took a sip of the coffee and grimaced. "The coffee here still tastes like despair."

"The more things change, the more they stay the same, right?"

Beth sat at the empty station and sipped her coffee. She didn't really know how she was going to observe what was happening around her. The contact center employees were speaking into their headsets, and she couldn't hear much of what they were saying.

She decided to start with the spot she was sitting in. The person who usually sat there had put up some pictures of their family on the low wall on one side of the station. Two kids, both girls, appeared in several pictures, obviously taken at successive ages. In one picture, they were on a beach, in another, in front of a Christmas tree. A schedule of last season's Phillies games was tacked up next to the pictures. Several sticky notes were attached to the monitor. One featured a hand-drawn smiley face and the instruction "SMILE!" The sticky note attached below read in tiny handwriting, "even if you really are not feeling it." Another note stated, "It's 5 o'clock somewhere!" with a picture of a martini glass.

The buzz in the room had picked up considerably. She noticed that all the employees were now taking calls, and the large monitor at the front of the room became more active, flashing green and red icons.

Mo came over to her. "Do you see it?"

"What?" The visual display had been put in six months ago, and although she had been involved in approving it, and had come into the contact center on the day it was launched, she had to admit she didn't understand what it was communicating.

"Customers are abandoning their call. It is only 7:30 a.m., and seven customers who have been put on hold have hung up. They will probably call back, but they won't be happy."

"How can you tell that?"

Mo walked with her over to the display. "See that red square flashing there? That indicates that calls have been abandoned in the last 10 minutes. I know it is seven because it says seven over here, which shows cumulative abandoned calls for the shift. A couple of minutes ago, before the volume picked up, it was 0." He pointed to the other side of the board. The "7" blinked for a second and changed to an "8."

Beth was impressed. They had demonstrated the board on the day she had visited, but she hadn't paid much attention to it when she visited the contact center after that.

"What do you do about that?" she asked.

"When the associates see the red square indicating that calls are being abandoned, they are supposed to reduce their call handling time from 4 minutes to 3 minutes. That should help reduce the call wait time for other customers and reduce call abandons – when a customer hangs up before their call is answered." Mo pointed to another set of numbers. "But as you can see, the calls are not being closed within 4 minutes, never mind, 3 minutes."

"Wow," Beth said. "When I started in the contact center, we were supposed to handle calls in 8 minutes."

Mo smirked. "Welcome to the future! That would be a luxury we can't afford. We just have too much call volume to spend that amount of time on calls. Except right now, our Average Handling Time is up to 7 minutes, and we have had many calls last more than 20 minutes. That is why I need more help."

Beth felt a surge of embarrassment. "Mo, I had no idea how challenging things were here. I wish you had brought this up in our one-on-one meetings."

"Well, to be fair, we haven't had a one-on-one in several weeks. You and I have both been swamped. On the other hand, I have given you some hints."

"That's true, and I'm sorry I didn't pay better attention. Roberta is clear about no budget for additional heads. We're going to have to get creative."

Mo was usually cheerful and friendly, but now he was scowling. "They seem to have money for this new lean initiative. There are consultants and coaches all over the place."

"I guess that will run its course. I'm getting a coach, by the way. Maybe I can get them to take a few calls!"

Beth wondered what to do next. "Mo, is there someone who would be comfortable with me listening in on a call or two?"

The smile returned to Mo's face. "I was ready for that. Julie would be happy to let you listen in."

PRACTICE THIS TODAY

What systems are you using to identify problems? What metrics? In what ways are they helpful? In what ways are they not helpful?

Chapter 5

Carlo's New Office

"Hey, Carlo!"

Carlo looked up from his laptop and saw Brandon rounding the corner into the cafeteria. Brandon sat down at the table across from Carlo. "Is this your office now?"

Carlo looked around. "I kind of like it here. I do have a cubicle assigned to me, but this is better. Nice windows, as much coffee as I need all day, and I get to see all the comings and goings. I like a little buzz in the background. And Linda stops in here a lot too, so it's easy to keep up to speed with what she is working on."

"Your way of going to the *gemba*, huh?"[1]

"You could say that. Hey, so what did your team think of that meeting?"

Brandon smiled. "We're throwing a lot at them. Lean, CPS, new strategy. I got some pushback afterwards about how they are not all that creative, and they don't see how this works. But not from everyone. Roberta was very excited, and a couple of the others."

Brandon took off his glasses. "Don't let me leave these here. I think I need more information about CPS to answer their questions. A lot of them are very pragmatic and logical, and not so idealistic in their approach. Just the word 'creative' makes them nervous."

"Hmm. I have found that even the most pragmatic person is more often swayed by emotion than fact, but I'd be happy to give you some science behind CPS." Carlo pulled a piece of paper out of his folder, in case he needed to draw. He looked up at Brandon. "Are those new glasses?"

"Uh huh. Readers. I guess that goes with becoming a CEO."

"Do you mind me asking how old you are?"

"Thirty-five. Which is young for readers. And young for a CEO, I guess."

"So, you're not too old to remember being a kid. Do you have any children?"

A warm smile spread over Brandon's face. "Yes, two. A little girl just turning 3 and a 6-month-old baby boy. They are amazing. Tiring, but amazing. This is all for them – keeping the business going and growing."

Carlo nodded. "A powerful incentive to turn things around. That is beautiful. Tell me about your baby boy. Six months is a wonderful age. Is he a learning expert?"

"I would say so. Six months ago, he was just completely dependent on us. And now he can sit up, he can engage people – he 'flirts' with everyone he meets, he is babbling, and he …" Brandon stopped. "I can go on and on about him. And about my daughter."

"And you're within your rights to do that," Carlo replied. "Dads are supposed to be proud. But, look, it's not just your kids, as wonderful as they are. It's what all humans are good at: learning. From the moment we're born, we're learning experts. In around a year, we learn to walk, and probably run. In a few more months toddlers master enough of their native language to become a typical troublesome 2-year-old, able to demand things, make arguments, and get what they want – most of the time! Their curiosity is boundless. They touch everything, taste everything – right? And they experiment continually."

"They do. That's what makes them tiring!"

"Have you ever wondered what is happening as their brains develop? They store memories, impressions, and experiences in their brains – the chocolate tastes good, the stove is hot."

Brandon interrupted. "My daughter was more cautious than my son."

"Her brain was still soaking up memories and experiences. Just a different personality type."

"That is for sure," replied Brandon.

"As babies experiment and learn, their brains work continuously to use any negative memories and experiences to bolster the natural defense mechanisms that evolution gave them to stay alive. This is the science part, by the way. Deep within every human's brain, a tiny region called the amygdala retains negative memories. These negative memories, like the time you touched a hot stove, or when someone yelled at you, are used to trigger the so-called 'fight or flight' response, to protect you from danger."

The "fight or flight" response is intended to protect us from danger.

Brandon mused out loud. "I've heard that the fight or flight response is a 'primitive' response, that we don't need much now we live far away from animals that can eat us."

"That is a good way to think of it, though we still need it sometimes. And you can often tell it is happening by physical changes. Your mouth gets dry, your heart races, you might feel a twinge in your gut, or even nausea as your digestion slows down. When it is triggered, we still want to fight things or run away from them. You should know that the fight or flight response can also be triggered by unfamiliarity of any kind. A new dish, a potential job change, a new idea, can all result in a rush of hormones that we associate with discomfort. If your gut is telling you that an idea is a bad idea, it may not really be your gut – but your amygdala, which has triggered adrenaline to course through your circulation and slow your digestion down!"

"And the impact of that on our creativity would be negative, right?" asked Brandon.

"Yes, because creativity and innovation are all about newness, and we can be wired to avoid, or try to kill, or run away from newness. It's not a bad character trait, by the way, and it can be overcome, when it interferes with creativity."

Carlo continued. "Think about your little boy. Does he like to drop things from his highchair?

"Oh yes, he does. Our dog is getting fat!"

"Your son is being a scientist, testing that gravity works on all objects, and testing to see what your response is, and probably the dog's as well. What is happening in that little head?"

"More brain science?"

"Yes, more brain science. When a child or an adult is engaged in creative learning activities, another area of the brain, the prefrontal cortex, is highly active, and the chemicals that are released cause pleasant sensations. Your son is learning, and being creative, and he is also getting a good feeling, good sensations, when he does that. Sometimes I feel as if adults, in their routines, don't experience that as much."

"Not when I'm dealing with my emails, or the financial spreadsheets, but I do know what that feels like."

"When does that happen, Brandon?"

"Well, you might not believe this of a CEO of a plumbing supply company, but I'm a pretty good bass guitar player. I don't get to play much anymore, kids, and work and all, but when I was in a band and we were working up a new set – that was great. Time flew by, and I would feel almost, you know, high."

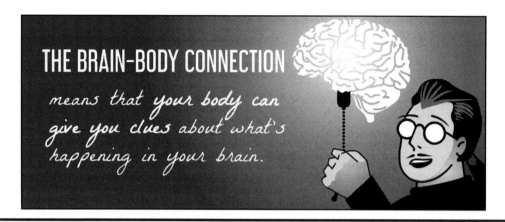

THE BRAIN-BODY CONNECTION *means that your body can give you clues about what's happening in your brain.*

Figure 5.1 The Brain-Body Connection.

"I'm glad you can express that. If you pay attention to how your body feels, you can gain some insight into what is happening in your brain."

"For your pragmatic colleagues, understanding something about the interplay between the amygdala, the prefrontal cortex and other regions of the brain will help them understand how to build patterns that lead to innovation, even in highly uncertain circumstances. The tools of Creative Problem Solving will allow you to learn to keep your thinking in the prefrontal cortex, so you can generate ideas, listen to other people's ideas, and choose ideas to carry forward."

Brandon took the piece of paper that Carlo had ready to draw on and made some notes on it. "Would it be fair to tell my pragmatists that the tools of CPS help them to be more creative?"

Creative Problem Solving tools help you become more creative.

"You could, although there is more to becoming more creative than just using a set of tools. The tools set you on the right path."

"What else is needed?"

"You can help by giving your brain opportunities for making connections and reaching insights, things like walking outside, stepping away from the problem you're trying to solve, using meditation and mindfulness practices. You might find that getting back to your guitar playing will help too."

Time away from the problem gives your brain space to make connections and reach insights.

"That might be a little too 'woo-woo' for them," said Brandon with a mischievous smile.

"Little by little, we'll get there. But you can make progress by feeding your brain a wide range of information to make connections with. Outside interests and hobbies are very important. Do you encourage your employees to take time for themselves? You can help by showing interest in and valuing their growth outside of work."

> To improve creativity, feed your brain a wide variety of information.

"And here's another piece of science. In a study, the brains of rappers were scanned while they were 'freestyling.' Most of the areas of the brain that are involved in decision-making appeared to be dormant, while the medial prefrontal cortex, which usually gets little day-to-day use, was highly activated. That gives us a clue about when to make decisions – and it's not when we're trying to think creatively. So, we're right when we separate divergent thinking from convergent thinking."

"This was helpful, Carlo," said Brandon. "Can I come see you in your 'office' another time?"

"You bet," said Carlo. "Any time."

PRACTICE THIS TODAY

Recall a time when you did not respond well to a new idea or a change in your life. What did you feel physically? Now think about a time when you were completely engaged in learning or creating something new. How did you feel? What do you do to expand your knowledge outside of your work environment? How might you enrich your learning outside of work?

Note

1. *Gemba* is a Japanese word meaning the actual place where work is done.

Chapter 6

Listening into Calls

Mo took Beth to meet Julie. Beth had met her several times before and knew that Mo considered her to be one of his best employees. They waited while Julie completed a call and entered information about the call into the computer.

"Julie, as I explained earlier, Beth is going to listen into a few of your calls. She is not evaluating you; I just want her to hear the kinds of issues we have been having in the past couple of weeks." He indicated where Beth was to sit and attached an additional headset to the phone. "Beth, please check that your headset is muted on each call."

Beth reached out to shake Julie's hand. "Thank you for letting me do this." Julie shook her hand quickly and turned her attention to an incoming call. She smiled as she greeted the customer.

"Good morning, Global Plumbing Supply, my name is Julie Jacobs. May I have your name, please?"

The caller didn't sound happy. "Richard Krauss. Need me to spell that?"

"Yes, please."

"K-R-A-U-S-S. Richard."

"And do you have a customer number?"

"1536943344." Julie entered the number into the computer. Beth could see the customer's account information appear on the screen.

"How may I help you today?"

"You can tell me where my order is. I ordered several parts four days ago, and they didn't arrive on the truck again this morning. I don't know what is up with you folks, but I can't keep my customers waiting like this."

Julie's voice stayed calm. "One moment please while I review this issue. May I put you on hold?"

"Sure. But I don't have all day."

Julie scrolled through the display on her screen. "Beth, look at this. Do you see a recent order?"

Beth squinted at the monitor. "It looks like his last order was two weeks ago. I'm not seeing anything more recent."

Julie returned to her caller. "Mr. Krauss, do you have an order number?"

"Yeah, I guess so. I ordered with that new app."

"It should be in a confirmation email you received when you completed the order."

"Okay, hang on. How do I look at my email when I'm talking on the phone?"

"I don't know what kind of phone you're using, sir, but you can usually open other apps and keep the call in the background."

"Oh hell."

"Mr. Krauss, I have your phone number as 267–555–3733. Is that correct?"

"Yeah."

"I can call you back if we get disconnected."

They heard some beeps and a muffled curse. "Okay, I got into my email. I'm not seeing a confirmation email."

"Please check your junk or spam folder."

"Nope. Nothing. What does that mean?"

"Sir, I believe the order was not completed using the app. We don't have a record of it here. I would be happy to expedite an order for you if want to make the order over the phone."

"You're telling me that the parts are not on their way? How the hell did that happen?"

"If you give me the part numbers you need now, you will have them tomorrow."

"I don't need them tomorrow! I need them two days ago! You idiots and your stupid app! I'm losing money here!"

"Sir, please calm down. I will do my best to help you." Julie's voice was still calm and friendly.

"Yeah, well, you suck and your app sucks and your company sucks. You're not going to help me anymore."

The line went dead.

Beth looked at Julie who was entering information into the computer. "Wow. That went bad fast."

Julie grimaced. "Less than three minutes! Good call handling time, right? But not a happy customer."

"What are you going to do?"

"Me? I just take the next call. Mr. Krauss is Mo's problem now." Julie pressed a button on her phone and smiled.

"Good morning, Global Plumbing Supply, this is Julie Jacobs. May I have your name, please?"

PRACTICE THIS TODAY

Are you or your employees locked into standardized actions and responses that don't bring satisfaction to customers? How might you bring creative thinking to your standardized processes?

Chapter 7

Beth Meets the Coaches

Beth went to Roberta's office at 10 a.m., as requested, an extra-large coffee in hand. She had not slept well. Snippets of the day in the contact center kept running through her mind. She felt mortified that she hadn't known how difficult things were in the contact center, despite Mo's "hints" and requests for more help. The problems with the on-line app were worse than she had anticipated, and despite the professionalism of the contact center staff, it was clear that they were losing the confidence of their customers.

She was surprised to see not one, but two people sitting and chatting with Roberta at the large oval table that Roberta used as a desk. She hesitated outside the open door, but Roberta called her into the office, and invited her to sit down.

"Beth, I'd like you to meet your new coaches." Roberta indicated the tall gray-haired woman. "This is Linda Lomax, your lean coach, and this gentleman is Carlo Cox, your CPS coach."

Beth was speechless. She was already not happy at being told that she "needed coaching" and needing two coaches was almost more than she could believe. Still, she wasn't going to let on her consternation, so she shook each coach's hand, and said she was pleased to meet them.

Roberta seemed to be genuinely happy.

"Beth, your area is key to our improvement. I've been thinking about how to quickly build your skills as a lean leader and I'm just thrilled that Carlo and Linda are available to work with you while I'm building my own skills working with the sales groups. They have been wonderful coaches and thinking partners to me in the past couple of weeks, so I feel you're in great hands. Linda and Carlo, I know you will enjoy working with Beth."

Linda spoke first. "I realize this is quite unusual, to have two coaches. Carlo and I are good friends and colleagues and we have complementary skill sets to share with you. It won't be the same as being coached by your manager, and, frankly, Carlo and I might not always agree, but we will always be focused on you and your development. Sometimes we will meet one-on-one, and there may be times when all three of us meet, or even all four us, including Roberta. We'll do our best to meet your schedule and your needs."

Carlo picked up the conversation. He looked a little younger than Linda, and although he was dressed in the business casual office uniform of a polo shirt and khakis, Beth noticed that he had specks of what looked like oil paint on his hands, and his hair was gathered in a neat ponytail. "You may be wondering why Roberta wants you to have a Creative Problem Solving coach as well as a lean coach. Linda and I think it is cool that Roberta wants you to learn lean and the CPS tools. She must think a lot of you to make this investment!"

Roberta leaned forward. "Beth, that is true. And I could leave you with Linda alone and you'd be in good shape. But our business really needs creative thinking and innovation, and I have found CPS to add a lot of value to lean thinking. This is kind of an experiment, and I appreciate you being willing to give it a try. At least, I hope you're willing to give it a try."

Linda chuckled. "Well, that's very lean of you, Roberta, to look at this as an experiment. And kind of you, Beth, to participate!"

Roberta leaned back in her chair. "Beth, what questions do you have?"

"Roberta, I appreciate your interest in my development, I really do. But things are chaos right now. I don't have time for coaching – never mind two coaches."

Roberta looked a little stunned. "As you can see, you can always count on Beth for an honest and heartfelt response."

The two coaches smiled sympathetically. Linda leaned in toward Beth. "Coaching is a two-way street, Beth. Yes, you will need to put time into the coaching sessions and into work that the sessions may indicate. I assure you that Carlo and I will work with you to make sure that what you're learning and developing is directly applicable to the problems you're trying to solve. We will never tell you an answer, but we will help you frame and understand the problems and find good solutions."

"Creative solutions!" added Carlo.

Linda continued. "Ultimately, it is your choice, not Roberta's as to whether you agree to this arrangement. You will always be in the driver's seat."

Figure 7.1   Coaching.

Roberta stood up. "I think Beth should try this for a week or two, and then decide. She doesn't know what she is objecting to."

Beth saw Linda make a note in her notebook.

"It is still Beth's decision," Carlo said. "Beth, just so you know, while Roberta is the sponsor in this arrangement, our conversations will not be shared with her. Unless there is something you would like to be shared. And, please, if there are questions you would like to ask without Roberta in the room, we can arrange that."

Strangely, Roberta did not appear to be bothered by Carlo's statement. She was standing by the door, awaiting a decision from Beth.

"No, it's fine," said Beth. "We can do a couple of weeks as an experiment, right? When do we start?"

Linda handed her a slip of paper. "I am teaching an Introduction to Lean Thinking class next week. It meets every morning from 8 to 12. We will start the coaching the week after."

"Every day next week?" Beth looked at Roberta. "Am I expected to attend every session?"

Linda also looked at Roberta.

Roberta's face looked more like the "old Roberta." She was losing patience. "Participation in coaching is your decision, Beth, but training is not. I expect you to be there."

Beth thought of all the meetings, emails, conference calls on her calendar next week. It was going to mean long days of catching up once she got home every night.

"I'll be there," she said.

PRACTICE THIS TODAY

As you go through your day, notice how often you make "judgment calls." Do you think you're stopping your own creative ideas before they have a chance? Are you missing opportunities?

Linda says that coaching is a two-way street. What does that mean to you? Who is coaching you? Who are you coaching?

Chapter 8

Beth's First Coaching Session

Beth was right. Attending the lean training class set her work schedule back considerably. The sessions themselves were interesting, and Linda did a good job of keeping the training focused and fun, but the emails kept coming in, multiple meetings had to be rescheduled, and Beth felt guilty about not helping Mo with the problems in the contact center. By the end of the week, she began to wonder whether any of the topics covered in the class could be applied at Global Plumbing Supply. Linda stressed the need for leaders to be "at the *gemba*" with their employees and for improvement to become a daily habit. Beth just didn't see how she could squeeze visits to the areas she supervised, daily stand-up meetings, and multiple improvement projects into her packed schedule.

This meant that she missed Connor scoring a goal in his soccer game on Saturday because she was looking at email on her phone, and she stayed up late Sunday night trying to figure out budget issues that made no sense to her. By Monday, when she sat down with Linda and Carlo for her first coaching session, she was feeling stressed and uncooperative.

They met in Roberta's office (Roberta was at an off-site meeting). Linda was already there when Beth arrived, but Carlo was not. Linda and Beth made small talk until Carlo appeared, carrying three cups of coffee.

"Looks like we're ready to start." Beth said, as soon as Carlo sat down.

"Great!" said Linda and Carlo together. They looked at each other and started laughing.

"We'd better stick to one person talking at a time," said Carlo, perhaps picking up on Beth's lack of amusement. "Linda, why don't you go first?"

"Agreed." said Linda. "Beth, our meeting today is essentially a contracting meeting. In this meeting, we will hear your goals for this coaching engagement, what our mutual responsibilities will be, work out logistical details like how and when we should meet."

"I don't understand," said Beth. "I thought Roberta contracted you."

Linda smiled. "That is true, Roberta is the sponsor of this engagement, and Carlo and I have contracts that describe our business relationship with Roberta and your company. Also, we want to make sure that the work we do with you meets *your* needs, so we're going to contract that with you today. We think it will help us all to have that clarity." Linda turned to Carlo. "Carlo, do you want to add anything?"

"No, I'm all for clarity."

Linda turned to Beth again. "Beth, what are your goals for the coaching?"

Beth grimaced "Can I be honest?"

"We like honesty as much as we like clarity," said Carlo. "Right, Linda?"

"Go for it, Beth," Linda responded.

"This coaching seems like a real added burden right now. My goal would be to have it take as little time as it can and for it to disrupt my work as little as possible. I'm flattered that Roberta wants me to be coached – at least I think I'm flattered, and I do very much want to develop as a leader, but I can't think of a worse time for this to be added to my plate."

Linda smiled at Beth. "Beth, I think you're fantastic!" Carlo was nodding his head. "I think I can speak for Carlo when I say that we're deeply appreciative of your honesty, and your trust in sharing that with us."

Carlo nodded his head in agreement again. "I completely concur with that. And please be assured, as we said when we first met, that we will not share the content of our conversations with Roberta."

Linda leaned forward. "What did you think of the lean training?"

"Well, I thought it was pretty interesting, and a lot of it makes sense, and I would love to see lean happen here, but given how difficult things are right now, I feel the same way about the lean stuff as I do the coaching. It seems like a big burden to add to everything else that is going on."

"Thank you for that!" said Linda. "Was there anything you learned that seemed as if it could be helpful?"

"Hmm, I liked the way you talked about lean leadership. I wish we had more leaders who thought that way. You know, who are focused on supporting and developing their people so their people can focus on solving problems. I aspire to that sort of leadership, but a lot of stuff gets in the way."

Carlo opened a notebook. "Can you tell us more?"

"In the training, Linda talked a lot about how lean is about reducing waste in the organization and increasing customer value, and that the best way to do that is have the people who are doing the work solve the problems that cause the waste. That means that their leader's job is to coach them to see and solve the problems. But that's not how my job as a leader works."

"For example?" prodded Carlo.

"For example, in the training, Linda talked about the importance of going to where the work is actually happening. But my time is so limited that I rarely have the chance to do that." Beth stopped and thought for a few moments. "I did have a chance do that, the week before last. I spent the day in the contact center, and I have to say I learned a lot. But I didn't really know what to do with what I learned, and I didn't see how me being there helped the employees. I think I made some of them nervous. And then I missed a day of other work I should have been doing, and then I got even more behind because I went to the lean training, so I haven't followed up on that visit."

Carlo nodded. "Interesting." He leaned back in his chair and looked at the ceiling for a moment. "I heard you say you aspire to 'that kind of leadership.' I also heard you say that there is a lot of stuff stopping you right now. Is that fair?"

"Yes, I guess so."

"I wonder if this might be a goal for our coaching sessions: 'It would be great if Beth were a leader who is able to help her employees see and solve problems.'"

"That sounds kind of, you know, lofty! How many sessions do we have anyway?"

Carlo laughed. "You're honest, and practical. Bear with me for a few minutes, because I want to explore this potential goal with you and Linda."

He handed Beth a stack of sticky notes and a black marker. Linda chuckled. "I think that is a world record, even for you, for bringing out the sticky notes!"

Carlo pushed a stack of the yellow notes toward Linda. "You can play too." He stood up and wrote on Roberta's whiteboard. "It would be great if Beth were a leader who is able to help her employees see and solve problems."

"Okay, Beth and Linda, what do you see as a plus, a good thing about that goal? Write it on a sticky note."

Beth thought for a moment, and then wrote in small letters at the top of a sticky note: "Roberta will be happy I have a goal." She put the black marker down. She noticed that Linda had already written about five stickies. "Good start, Beth," Carlo observed. "What else?"

Beth picked up the black marker and wrote on the same sticky note: "I already have goals for this year."

Carlo noticed what she was doing. "Oh, apologies, Beth, I should have told you that I want each plus on a separate sticky. Please re-write that on a new sticky."

Beth crossed the statement out. "It wasn't so much of a plus."

"That's cool," replied Carlo. "You can keep it for when we do issues. For now, let's focus on pluses. What else?"

Beth opened and closed the black marker several times. Finally, she picked up a clean sticky note and wrote: "Coaching will be more useful because it will be focused on a goal I care about." Carlo picked up her two pluses and the eight or nine that Linda had jotted down and stuck them on the whiteboard. "I'm going to read these out loud, as they may spur other ideas." As he read Beth's and Linda's contributions, Beth felt her mood begin to lift. Although it was hard to think up the pluses, and she couldn't do it as fast as Linda, hearing Linda's ideas helped her think about more positive attributes of the goal. She jotted down a couple more and then grabbed another sticky and wrote: "I might be able to save the contact center."

Carlo picked it up and read it out loud. "That is more of an opportunity but let's go there. What opportunities might this goal bring about? What could it lead to?"

Beth was surprised that Carlo didn't comment on the audaciousness of her statement, but quickly wrote down another opportunity. "We could have happy customers." Carlo placed the note on the whiteboard. "What else?"

Beth started to feel excited. She wrote: "I could get a promotion" and "The contact center could be a benchmark for the rest of the company." She realized she hadn't thought much about the warehouse. "The warehouse might be a better place to work." Carlo continued to read the opportunities out loud and place the sticky notes on the whiteboard. After several minutes, both Beth and Linda had stopped writing. Half of the whiteboard was covered in neatly aligned sticky notes under the headings "Pluses" and "Opportunities."

Linda looked expectantly at Carlo. "Issues?"

"Yes, issues. Beth, now is the time to bring back that problem you wanted to raise. I'd like you to write it down in a very specific way. Please state it like this: 'How might we?' or 'How to?' or 'What are all the ways that?'"

"Like this? 'How might I deal with the fact I already have a full set of goals?'"

Carlo nodded. "Very good. Write it down like that." Again, Beth was surprised. She had expected an argument from Carlo or Linda when they heard her issue with the goal, but so far, neither one had commented positively or negatively on anything she had said or written down.

She wasn't surprised, however, when Carlo asked, "What else?"

It wasn't long before the whiteboard blossomed with sticky notes under the heading "Issues." Even though Beth was now allowing all her negative thoughts about lean and coaching to come to mind – and get written down – she still felt energized. Perhaps it was the freedom of being able to articulate her thoughts, or the lack of judgment from her coaches – she wasn't sure.

When the writing slowed down again, Carlo invited her to review the issues. "Beth, please look at everything that is up here and pick the issues that are the most important to you. You can draw a star on your key issues. Take your time."

Beth walked up to the whiteboard, a black marker in hand. She read every sticky note. Finally, she picked four and drew stars on them.

- How might we deal with the fact I already have a full set of goals?
- What are all the ways I can make time for coaching?
- What are all the ways I can make time for going to the *gemba*?
- How might I learn to coach my employees when I'm not an expert on any of this?

"Any others?" asked Carlo.

Beth looked at the whiteboard again. "Yes, this one: 'How might I learn to trust Roberta?'"

"Let's add it," said Carlo. "What do you think about that goal we started with? Do you want to edit or update it?"

"Yes, I do. How about this? *'It would be great if Beth were a lean leader who created trust so that her employees and supervisors could see and solve problems.'*"

Carlo finally allowed himself a moment of judgment. "That's deep, Beth. That's deep. Wow, you're going to be awesome to work with."

Figure 8.1 Lean Leadership.

Linda nodded. "I agree, that is a deep and inspiring goal. One that means that you will need to go beyond lean tools and CPS tools, because what you're aiming for is a change in mindset."

"A change in mindset? That sounds hard."

"Indeed," said Linda.

"Which is a perfect segue into new thinking," said Carlo. "New thinking. Beth, each of these issues you have chosen are problems that you will work on solving, with our support."

"And Roberta's," added Linda. "We'll all work with you to understand these problems and use new thinking to come up with and test solutions."

Beth's phone buzzed. "Hey, I'm sorry, I have to run. Did we get to what you wanted, to contract with me?"

"Not completely," Linda replied. "We'll finish at our next meeting. How are you feeling about all this?"

Beth smiled. "Weirdly good. I feel like I have gotten myself into something huge. But it's good. Weirdly good."

PRACTICE THIS TODAY

Think again about who is your coach and who you are coaching. What are the benefits of coaching, both for the coachee and the coach?

Why did Beth feel more positively about her "issues" when they were phrased as questions?

Chapter 9

Getting to the POINt

After Beth left the room, Linda looked at Carlo quizzically. "Carlo, what did you just do? You somehow took Beth through a thought process that helped her overcome her initial objections to being coached to becoming a lean thinker and leader."

"You caught me! The steps that I went through are found in a creative problem-solving tool called POINt.[1]

There was a little space left on the whiteboard and Carlo used it to write down the steps of POINt.

Carlo pointed at the whiteboard as he spoke. "POINt is an elegant tool that fosters thinking that must done in the frontal lobes. POINt is designed to evaluate and develop ideas, or proposals or options. We often apply it to

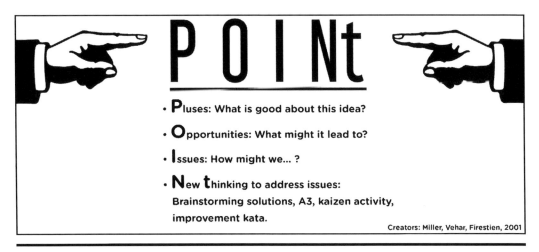

Figure 9.1   POINt.

evaluating or developing solutions. The 'plusses,' 'opportunities,' and 'issues' serve to evaluate the proposal. The new thinking is all about strengthening it. Here are the steps I followed.

"I started with a proposal for the goal of the coaching sessions, which was a recapitulation of Beth's desire – in other words, although I articulated and wrote down the coaching goal, I only wrote what I heard Beth say."

"A good coaching practice," commented Linda.

"I then asked Beth and you to state 'Pluses.' A plus is anything, anything at all, positive about the idea. If you're used to doing SWOT (Strengths, Weaknesses, Opportunities, Threats) analysis, think about the 'strengths' of the idea or proposal."

"But this didn't feel painful the way SWOT can feel. You stayed on the positive side of things."

"Right, unlike a SWOT analysis, POINt's next step is Opportunities. A good way to spur the generation of opportunities is to use a sentence starter like 'It might,' or 'It could lead to.'"

Linda interjected. "Why move to Opportunities and skip the Weaknesses?"

"Linda, that is a good question, and it reveals the purpose of POINt. As we ponder opportunities, we must engage our imaginations, which requires us to keep our thinking in the 'higher' parts of the brain. As we listen to the pluses and opportunities, we can become engaged in the idea or proposal, and become open to change, and our ability to ideate is freed. The key principle is 'Praise First.'"

> Using "Praise First" is the key to not saying "no" immediately.

"But of course, every idea or proposal has shortcomings. And you did get to them."

"Right. In POINt, the Issues are considered: but they are listed in a way that invites problem solving. Issues are stated as questions: 'How might we?' or 'What are all the ways?' We stay in the part of the brain that is generative and innovative.

"What we ran out of time to do with Beth is 'New Thinking.' Each critical issue is treated as a problem to be solved."

"And that is something we can address with lean problem solving," Linda pointed out.

"Exactly, but listen, in POINt as described by Miller, Vehar and Firestien, this involves brainstorming potential solutions to the issues."

"Mm ... in a lean environment, this might also mean that an issue becomes the subject of a kaizen workshop (small or large), an A3, and/or a set of improvement katas."

"I want to talk about how to incorporate creative thinking into each of those approaches," offered Carlo.

"Oh, we will! That is one of the things that keeps me excited about working with you. Let me summarize about POINt to make sure I understand it. The elegance of POINt lies in its impact on the human brain. POINt drives thinking to the frontal lobes. Even when issues are raised, they are treated as problems to be solved, not judgments to kill ideas or proposals."

Carlo nodded in agreement. "You got it. Remember, 'Praise First.' For many people, POINt is a completely foreign way of thinking. In my early training, I was taught to look for the flaws in an idea or hypothesis first. And in business ... have you experienced this? Someone will present an idea or proposal (usually with a lengthy PowerPoint presentation). If they are lucky, they will get to the second or third slide before someone (often a senior leader) will raise 'questions.' The questions are rarely legitimate questions; they are objections or issues. The presenter may go into a defensive mode, sometimes resorting to back-up slides to address the issues. If there is no pertinent back-up slide, they are viewed as unprepared. All parties walk away dreading the next meeting, and chances are, the attendees didn't even get to see the full proposal."

"In a lean environment, we try to avoid that kind of meeting, but I get your point (no pun intended)," Linda replied.

"Imagine a similar meeting using POINt as the agenda. The full proposal would be heard, and its attendees could highlight its positive attributes and the opportunities it creates. Then issues would be raised, as problems to be solved. If information, data, or solutions were available to address the issue immediately, great! If not, the magnitude of the issues and the work necessary to solve them could serve as input to a decision to move forward or not – or to charter work to solve the most critical issues. And all participants would walk away engaged and encouraged."

"This is good stuff, Carlo," said Linda. "We may be on to something here."

PRACTICE THIS TODAY

List five situations at work or home where you could practice using POINt.

Note

1. POINt was first described by Blair Miller, Jonathan Vehar, and Roger Firestien in *Creativity Unbound: An Introduction to Creative Process* (Williamsville, NY: Innovation Resources, Inc., 2001).

Chapter 10

Trouble in the Warehouse

After a few weeks, Beth began to look forward to her coaching sessions, at least the ones with Linda. Most of the time she met with Linda in person, "at the *gemba*" as Linda would say, and her meetings with Carlo took place on the phone. Every now and then, the three of them would meet. Looking back, Beth could see that things were starting to change for the better – except for the problems at the contact center. Roberta's opinion was that the IT department needed to fix the ordering app, and she directed Beth to work with the warehouse first. Beth, concerned about the stress levels in the contact center, protested, but Roberta was adamant. Keisha, who supervised the warehouse, had attended the lean training with Beth, and she was excited about making improvements.

Beth and Keisha decided that improvements in the warehouse could impact two of the company's goals:

- reduce safety incidents to 0.
- increase the operating margin to 10 percent.

Realizing that the company only made money when a customer received (and paid) for a part, Beth and Keisha started by working with the warehouse team to map the flow of parts from the time a part was ordered, to when it was dispatched to a plumbing company. They devoted a week to 5S[1] and discovered that a lot of space in the warehouse was taken up by parts that hadn't been requested in years. They measured how far the warehouse employees traveled to pick the most commonly used parts and at Beth's insistence, used the freed-up space from the 5S to create a supermarket[2] for the fast-moving parts. Linda showed them how to set up kanbans[3] so they stopped running out of key parts – this earned a lot of praise from their colleagues in the contact center, who noticed a decrease in call volume from customers wondering where a part was. They set up visual management tools in addition to the kanban signals in the supermarket: Progress boards showed the headway they were making in their improvement projects. Key performance indicators (KPIs) were displayed throughout the warehouse. Daily stand-up meetings in the warehouse, which had seemed impossible to cram into the schedule, now seemed easy – if Beth was off-site and missed them, she felt as if a piece of her day was missing. The number of emails coming into her inbox decreased, because she learned about problems earlier, and the employees were gaining confidence in solving problems in the warehouse.

In the coaching sessions with Linda, Beth was able to focus on her own behavior as a lean leader. She was learning to see what was happening in the warehouse and learning how to encourage Keisha and the warehouse employees to solve problems and be comfortable asking for help. She learned to ask more questions and listen more. For almost every situation they ran into in the warehouse, Linda had a lean tool to address it, and Beth eagerly encouraged the warehouse associates to adopt the tools.

Meanwhile, her conversations with Carlo were brief, and she began to wonder why she had to meet with him at all. She enjoyed her conversations with him, but they seemed to lack relevance to the work she was doing.

At the end of a coaching session with Linda, Linda announced that she was taking a few weeks off for a long-planned family vacation. Beth wasn't concerned, because the warehouse was running smoothly, and Beth believed that she and Keisha had enough lean knowledge to work on their own without coaching.

"Of course, Carlo is always available to you," Linda said in parting. "Remember to keep up with your stand-up meetings and updating your progress boards. I'm looking forward to seeing your progress when I get back!"

Three days later, Beth was awakened by her phone buzzing at 5 a.m. Keisha's name and smiling picture appeared on the screen.

"Hello? Beth?" Keisha sounded shaken.

"Hey, Keisha, it's 5 o'clock, what's wrong?"

"Beth, are you able to get over to work right now? I mean, I know you have to get Connor to school, but something has happened, and I need you here." Keisha's voice was trembling. "There's been a bad accident. Really bad."

"What happened? Are you okay?"

"I'm fine. I was just coming into the office when it happened. I didn't even see it, but I heard it."

"Hang on, I will be there as fast as I can. Call me back if you need to – I will keep the phone on." Beth jumped out of bed and pulled on a pair of jeans and a tee shirt. She woke Connor up, and told him that she had to leave for an emergency at work. She knew he would get himself up and on the bus. "Connor, please just remember to lock the door when you go, and don't forget to feed the cat."

"Before or after I lock the door, Mom?"

"Smartass!" She kissed him on the forehead. "Don't go back to sleep!"

Once she was in the car, she called Keisha back. "Hey, what happened?" In the background she heard a siren. "Is someone hurt?"

Keisha seemed a little calmer. "Yes, Tony was operating the forklift, and hit a shelving unit. I think the unit wasn't properly secured and collapsed. Tony is okay because of the forklift cage, but Judy was walking through the aisle and the unit fell on her. She was knocked unconscious. She's awake now, but she says she can't feel her legs. There is a helicopter on the way, and they are taking her to University Hospital."

"Oh, my God, what was she doing walking in the aisle while Tony was operating the forklift? And why wasn't the shelving unit properly secured?"

"I don't know, and I don't know. I have been stressing the importance of safety recently, and I have never seen anything like that when I have walked through the warehouse. I feel so responsible, but I don't know what went wrong!"

That morning started Beth's worst day at work. She had to call Roberta and Brandon, sit with Keisha and Tony as they explained what happened to the police and to the company safety officer, and worst of all, call Judy's husband and tell him that his wife was on her way to University Hospital in a helicopter. Roberta went to the hospital to be with him as Judy was evaluated and prepped for surgery.

Later, a lawyer came down to the warehouse offices and told Beth, Keisha, and the warehouse employees not to talk to anyone about the accident unless one of the company attorneys was present. Tony, the forklift operator, protested. "Why? Are you afraid Judy is going to sue? She should sue. Safety around here is a joke!" Beth saw Keisha stand up and walk out of the room. She found Keisha in the restroom.

"I'm not in here crying, if that's what you think," Keisha said angrily. "I just had to get away. I have been trying so hard to make safety a priority, and Tony just said it. It's not."

"What do you mean?" asked Beth. "It is one of the top company goals." She recalled Brandon standing in front of everyone at an all-hands meeting, proclaiming that "Zero Safety Incidents" was a goal everyone should take seriously.

"It's not like what we've done for improving warehouse operations. We've done all that work, mapping and doing 5S and creating the supermarket. We've made progress. But we assumed that talking about safety was enough. Supposing Judy does sue us? What will that do to our operating margin? But when we moved the shelving to make the supermarket, I didn't think to check that it was properly secured. And, apparently, people walking in the aisles while the forklifts are operating is done every day – just not when management is around to see it."

"But why?" asked Beth.

"Because we have increased the pick rate and people don't have the flexibility to wait for a forklift to be out of the aisle before they go in to pick a part."

Beth was surprised. "When did the pick rate get changed? That isn't in the metrics we reviewed."

Keisha pointed at herself. "I did that. I thought it would help our effectiveness. I didn't think it was important to tell you. And, Beth, you and I were at the *gemba*, but we didn't see what was really happening. And now Judy may never walk again."

"I don't get it," said Beth. "We told people it is safe to bring up problems and issues. We let them know it's okay. Why didn't they tell us? Why didn't you tell me about changing the pick rate?"

It was several hours later that Beth was finally able to sit down in her office and collect her thoughts. She desperately wanted to call Linda but knew that Linda was somewhere far away on a mountain top with no cell service. Roberta was still at the hospital with Judy's family, as Judy underwent a long and delicate surgery to fuse her spine.

Not being able to talk to Linda, she imagined what Linda might say to her.

"Beth, what is the problem you're trying to solve?" Beth wasn't sure. Was it making sure that shelving was properly secured, or something bigger? Employee engagement in safety? Employee trust that they could share issues?

Again, she imagined Linda's voice in her head. "What do you know about this problem?" That was hard to answer, because she wasn't clear about the problem.

"What is the goal of solving this problem?" Beth knew the answer to that – zero safety incidents.

"What is the problem you're trying to solve?" This was the question she kept coming back to. She knew Linda would ask her to plan a PDCA cycle, but without clarity on the problem, there was no point in doing any PDCA. In a way, there was no rush, because it would take several weeks for the safety officer to produce a report and start the corrective action process, but the new-found sense that as a manager she was truly responsible for other people's health and their very lives was weighing heavily on her. She glanced at her watch. It was almost 6 p.m., 13 hours since Keisha's call had woken her. She pulled out her phone and texted Connor, telling him to order pizza for dinner and do his homework. Then she dialed Carlo.

Carlo answered the phone immediately. "Hey, Beth, how are you? I saw your company mentioned on the news today. Is everyone okay?"

"No, we had a bad accident, and someone was seriously injured. I'm not really allowed to talk about it right now."

"I understand. What can I do to help you?"

"Well, don't take this the wrong way, I really felt I needed to talk to Linda, and she's on vacation. So, I called you."

Carlo chuckled. "That's okay. You've been doing a lot of good work with Linda, and you and I haven't had as much to talk about. But I'm here for you, and it's off the clock time today; don't worry about how long it takes."

"I have a problem, I mean, we, Keisha and Roberta, and me, and the whole company have a problem to solve, and I don't think that what I have learned so far about lean can help me solve it. I mean, maybe Linda would know something, but I'm stumped. And you know what, I'm going to have to talk about this accident a little bit."

She outlined the story in as general terms as she could. When she finished, she said, "I think Linda would tell me to start to plan a PDCA cycle to move forward. But this is not like solving a problem in the parts flow or setting some tools in order. I don't really know what the problem is, and I know I need to clarify it to get started."

Carlo listened. When she finished, he said, "Linda has taught you well. Do you mind if I do some teaching?"

"I guess I asked for it. So, yes, please."

"We've talked about the creative process. Do you remember what I call the heartbeat of the process?"

"Yes, alternating between divergent and convergent thinking."

"Right. Every step in the creative process has a phase when we do divergent thinking and a phase when we do convergent thinking. This rhythm applies to any problem-solving approach. So, in a PDCA cycle, we can feel that heartbeat as well.

"Roughly speaking, it goes like this:

"In the 'Plan' stage, you consider many possible actions; that is the divergent thinking. Then you select one or two to move forward – that is the convergent thinking. You also select from many possible ways to test the actions and select one experiment to run.

"In the 'Do' stage, you perform the action, do your experiment, as you planned it. You should have done all your divergent thinking in the Plan stage.

"In 'Check' or 'Study' you consider a range of meanings or implications from the results of your actions. That is divergent thinking again. Thinking convergently, you select the meanings that make the most sense. In the 'Act' or 'Adjust' stage, you consider a range of changes to your approach, and select the best to carry forward into your next PDCA cycle.

"Now sometimes, you don't need to think divergently and convergently in each stage. Sometimes the path forward or the adjustment to be made are clear. But if they are not, letting that creative heartbeat drive your thinking is vital. And it sounds to me as if you're in one of those unclear situations right now." Carlo paused. "I wish we were sitting together. I would love to draw you a picture. But I will send you one by email."

"I think I get it," said Beth. "In every stage but 'Do' we should consider a range of options and then select and strengthen how we move forward from that range of options."

"Yes, and don't forget, if you keep your experiments small, you can go back and test other options. You don't have to be right the first time."

"Linda would ask me, what problem am I trying to solve? Since I'm not sure, could I come up with several problem statements and then do some convergent thinking work to narrow them down and improve them?"

"What do you think?"

"I think, yes. I think it would be a good idea to do it with Keisha, and maybe some other people as well."

"Beth, I would be happy to come in and facilitate that work, if you would find it helpful. I'll discuss with Roberta."

"Carlo, thanks for listening – and thanks for teaching. I have a lot to think about."

PRACTICE THIS TODAY

What problems are you facing that don't have clear paths forward or well-known tools or best practices that might be good countermeasures? How do you usually address these problems?

Notes

1. 5S is an approach to organizing a workplace. The 5S are "Sort," "Set in order," "Shine," "Standardize," and "Sustain."
2. A "supermarket" contains an inventory or supplies organized for easy access. As the supplies are used, they are replaced.
3. Kanban (in the case of the supermarket) is a signal that the supplies or inventory need to be replenished.

Chapter 11

PDCA and CPS

After he hung up the phone, Carlo went to his notes from his discussions with Linda. He had learned from Linda that the Plan-Do-Check-Act cycle is intrinsic to lean thinking. Shorthand for the scientific method, and made a popular business concept by W. Edwards Deming, it breaks the usual mental paradigm of shuttling between planning and execution and forces us to learn as we make progress. Linda told him that some people think of the cycle as PDSA (Plan-Do-Study-Act) or even Allen Ward's product development learning cycle LAMDA (Look-Ask-Model-Discuss-Act).

As Carlo told Beth, sometimes a PDCA cycle is straightforward. But now when Beth was dealing with an unusual and poorly understood situation, he understood how challenging she found it to decide how to proceed.

Carlo realized that the CPS approach of separating divergent and convergent thinking would be extremely helpful. At its simplest, bringing the power of creativity to bear on challenging problems in each step of PDCA (except "Act") means asking:

> What are all the ...? (divergent thinking)

And

> Which few do we carry forward and how might we strengthen them ...? (convergent thinking)

He recalled a conversation he had had with Linda in his cafeteria "office."

"Do you remember me saying that PDCA is shorthand for the scientific method?" Linda had asked. "I have a confession about that. I think that the Plan stage in PDCA is too much of a shorthand representation of what happens in the scientific method."

"What do you mean?" Carlo had inquired.

"Think about how scientists really work. Plan includes:

1. Make an observation.
2. Create a hypothesis regarding the observation.
3. Design an experiment to test the observation.

Only after all those steps does a scientist conduct an experiment, which is what we call the 'do' step."

"From my perspective," Carlo had offered, "in each of these activities, there are opportunities for divergent and convergent thinking."

Now he thought about Beth's situation with the warehouse in this light. How might she plan and execute a PDCA cycle to clarify the problem she needed to solve, using creative thinking to enhance her lean thinking?

In their phone call, Beth had shared that she and Keisha had made several observations:

- Safety is one of the top company goals.
- Safety has been a communication focus.
- A terrible accident has happened.
- Tony stated that safety is not a priority.
- No one remembered to secure the shelving unit after it was moved to create the supermarket in the warehouse.
- No one checked that the shelving unit was secured.
- People have been walking in the aisles of the warehouse while the forklifts are in motion.
- Although Beth and Keisha try to be in the warehouse daily, they have not seen anyone walking in the aisles while the forklifts are moving.
- Keisha did not tell Beth that the pick rate had changed.
- No one told Beth or Keisha that the change in pick rate was leading people to violate safety rules.

Carlo knew that if Beth and Keisha and the warehouse team brainstormed on this, they would come up with other observations. But how would they know which observation or observations were most key? This required convergent thinking. Carlo forgot about his glass of wine as he started to write a facilitation plan for a meeting with Beth and Keisha.

PRACTICE THIS TODAY

Are you running some PDCA cycles? How might you use divergent and convergent thinking in your PDCA cycle?

Chapter 12

Doing and Checking and Adjusting without a Lean Coach

Carlo met with Beth and Keisha the next morning. The two managers had posted their observations about the previous day's event on the wall.

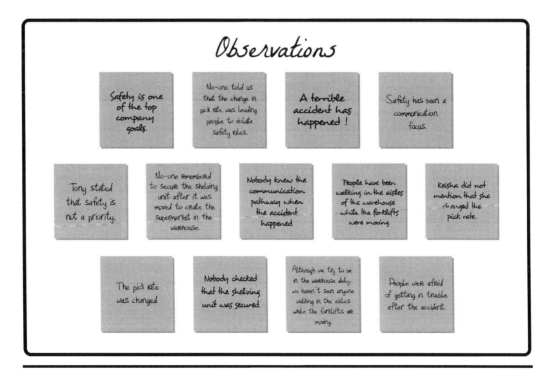

Figure 12.1 Observations.

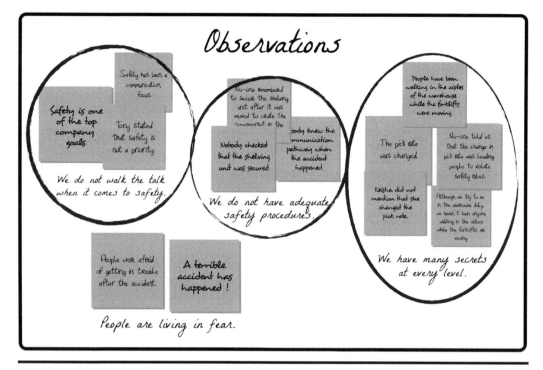

Figure 12.2 Observations Clustered and Named.

Once the observations were posted, Carlo asked Beth and Keisha to cluster them. Carlo asked them to discuss each observation before choosing to cluster it with others, to avoid clustering simply because statements contain similar words. "You should aim for clustering statements that have similar meanings, not similar words. Also, don't feel that you need to cluster every statement. The one that stands alone maybe will turn out to be the most important one!" he said.

After the observations have been clustered, they named each cluster (with a statement, not a single word or title). Finally, they voted to select the observation cluster to move forward.

Beth and Keisha chose to move forward with "We have many secrets at every level."

They also decided, after discussion, that the word "secrets" was not helpful, because "secrets" seemed to imply that people were withholding information deliberately and for bad purposes. They decided to rename the cluster "Why we don't tell."

Now what?" asked Beth. "We have an observation to move forward, so what comes next? A hypothesis?"

Figure 12.3 Cluster by Meaning.

"How about some divergent thinking to come up with some potential hypotheses for this observation?"

"Can we use the Five Whys?"[1] Beth had learned about the Five Whys in the lean training class.

"I'm worried," said Keisha, "that we haven't had any input from the people in the warehouse yet. Can we ask the Five Whys in a series of interviews? We could speak with people who work in the warehouse, and other people who interact with the warehouse personnel. We can share the observations in the 'Why we don't tell cluster' and ask why each person thought those observations came to be."

"Interesting idea," said Carlo. "Five Whys is often used to identify a single root cause, and so can be used as a tool for convergence."

Keisha considered this. "I think there might be more than one root cause for the problem of keeping and not sharing important information – or more than one belief as to why secrets should be kept. I believe interviews would reveal several potential root cases, or hypotheses to test."

"It's worth a try," said Beth.

After the interviews, they posted the results of the Five Whys on the whiteboard.

Once again, they used clustering to converge on some hypotheses to test. Because of the nature of the statements, it was especially important to

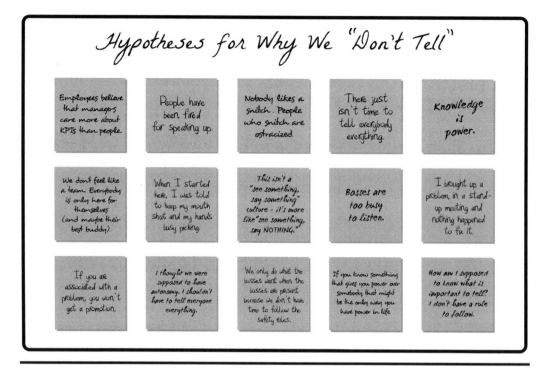

Figure 12.4 Hypotheses.

discuss the meaning of each statement before they clustered them. This took much longer than they expected, but the discussion was rich and helpful. "It occurs to me," said Beth, "that we are getting closer and closer to really understanding the current conditions. But it surprises me that it's taking so much effort for us to get to that understanding."

"Yeah," said Keisha in agreement. "I thought that I knew what was happening in my own department. I thought we'd be digging into solutions by now."

This time they did not vote on the cluster to move forward with. The conversation about the cluster "Managers demonstrate that KPIs are more important than safety" had been so passionate that everyone agreed that this would be the subject of their next experiment.

Now Beth and her team had gone through two cycles of divergent and convergent thinking to move from making observations to having a hypothesis to test (the "do" step) of the PDCA cycle. All they needed to do now was decide what experiment to run.

"Wow," said Beth, pushing her chair back from the table. "That was intense." The meeting to determine which hypothesis to take into the PDCA

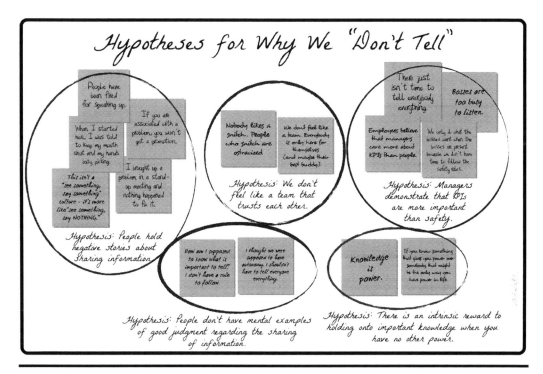

Figure 12.5 Hypotheses Clustered and Named.

cycle had just ended, and she, Keisha, Roberta, and Carlo were left in the room after the other members of the team had left. "I'm still shocked that despite all that 'going to the *gemba*,' we didn't see what was happening."

Roberta grimaced. "At least we got good news today about Judy. She is making great progress and she is headed to rehab next week."

"That is great to hear!" exclaimed Keisha. As the direct supervisor of the warehouse, she was carrying a large burden of guilt for what had happened to Judy.

"So, Carlo," said Beth. "We're ready to test our hypothesis. Well, almost ready, because I'm not clear what we're going to test, and how to test it."

"Your hypothesis is …"

"that managers demonstrate that KPIs are more important than safety," said Beth, finishing Carlo's sentence for him.

"In my CPS world, that sounds a lot like a problem that needs some more clarification."

"I agree it needs more clarification," Beth responded. "What I got from this whole exercise is that employees believe that managers demonstrate more interest in KPIs than safety. I just don't know why that is."

"So …" said Carlo. "What are all the ways you could find out why they believe that?"

He passed some sticky notes over to Beth.

"Do we have to do divergent thinking again?" asked Beth, only half-joking.

"Do you know how to find out why? If so, you don't need to think divergently. So, what is it: do you have an answer, or do you need to do more divergent thinking?"

Beth sighed, picked up the sticky notes and passed some to Keisha and Roberta. Unlike her first effort with divergent thinking, the ideas came to her easily, and she didn't try to judge them before she wrote them down. In a few minutes, they had a wall full of ideas. As usual, Beth had one more idea after she thought she had exhausted her imagination. Carlo called time and she quickly put it on the board.

"Roberta, would you like to select three of the ideas you think are promising? Sponsor's choice, but don't forget the guidelines for convergent thinking."

Roberta glanced up at the wall. The guidelines for divergent and convergent thinking were now posted in every conference room. "I will indeed be deliberate, check the objective, improve the ideas, be affirmative, and consider novelty."

"Great," said Carlo. "Go for it."

Roberta stood up, and carefully read every note on the wall. She went back and read a couple again, Finally, she pulled one sticky note off the wall and read it out loud. "Review meeting agendas and minutes from the last three months to see how much time is devoted to safety vs. KPIs." It was the very last sticky note that Beth had put on the board.

"Sponsor's choice," she said. "One is enough, and this one can be done fast. Once we see the results of this test, we can do some of the others if needed."

"Fair enough," said Carlo. "We will not lose these other ideas." He looked at the three managers. "How was that for quick divergence and convergence? You see, this doesn't have to be a lengthy exercise."

"Let's run the experiment," said Beth. "Maybe we can divide up the agendas and minutes between the three of us. Can we touch base tomorrow afternoon?"

Keisha shook her head. "I will do all of them. Then I can apply the same criteria to every document. Tomorrow afternoon is good."

The next day, the three managers met to review the results of Keisha's analysis. They dialed Carlo in on a teleconference line.

"It's pretty clear," Keisha announced, showing them a chart. "Safety is always mentioned at the beginning of each KPI review meeting, but when I looked at the rest of the agendas and minutes, almost none of the meeting time is spent on safety topics."

"What about KPIs?"

"Well, the warehouse folks are correct. They are advertised as KPI review meetings, so of course we spend a lot of time talking about KPIs. Eighty percent of the agenda topics are about KPIs."

Roberta looked at the chart. "Why don't we have safety KPIs? I mean, we have the company safety goal on Brandon's A3 – which obviously we're not going to achieve. We should have KPIs for safety like all the other metrics we review."

Beth cleared her throat. "Hang on a moment. I just want to pay attention to where we are in the PDCA process. We made some observations, we formulated some hypotheses to test, and we just ran an experiment. We have done 'Plan' and 'Do.' Let's think some more about the 'Check' step, before we move to 'Act.' "

Roberta gave her a sharp look, then smiled. "Thanks, Beth, I'm so used to making the decisions and moving things forward. But you have to give me credit – I asked a question!"

Carlo's voice crackled from the phone. "Beth, remember we said that 'Check' can have a divergent and a convergent phase? Where are you now?"

"I guess we could do some divergent thinking. 'Check' means to study the result of the experiment. I personally think that having some safety KPIs, like Roberta suggested are a good idea to explore, but let's think more deeply about what this result means."

"Creative thinking is deep thinking," Carlo remarked. "Once again, what is your hypothesis?"

Keisha answered. "That managers demonstrate that KPIs are more important than safety. I think the results of the experiment pretty much proved that."

"I agree," said Beth, "if the agendas are seen as what management thinks is important, then people could believe that managers demonstrate that we care more about KPIs than safety. But humor me for a minute – what other explanations might there be for this result?"

The three women sat and looked at each other for a moment. Nobody said anything.

"*If* people see these agendas as what management thinks is important," said Beth. "Is our next step another experiment to check that out?"

There was another period of silence. "Feeling stuck?" said Carlo from the phone. "What are all the ways you can find out if your employees take these agendas as indicating management priorities?"

"We could ask them," said Beth. "I mean, there are probably a lot of different ways to get to the bottom of this but asking them would be simple and fast. I know I asked for some divergent thinking, but now I feel as if we should just verify this one point."

"Let's do it," said Roberta. "Let's take that as our action."

"Carlo, I feel like we're letting you down, in some way," Beth said. "I mean, we didn't generate a lot of sticky notes."

"You did pause and consider before you implemented safety KPIs," said Carlo. "And, who knows, you might still do that. But by pausing and taking a moment to think more deeply, you may have saved yourselves a lot of wasted effort implementing safety KPIs that might not help. I'm very interested to hear what you learn from talking to people about these agendas."

The next afternoon, Beth, Keisha, and Roberta met again. They had each spoken with warehouse employees.

Beth spoke first. "My conversations were very interesting. Both the people I spoke to said that the meeting focus on KPIs did indicate to them that safety is not as important as meeting other goals. But they also said that they consider the meetings to be a show for management anyway."

"I got similar feedback," said Roberta. "I also heard that the questions we ask, 'at the *gemba*' are much more important to employees than what happens in the meeting."

"What did they mean by that?" asked Beth.

"They told me that when we're on the floor with them, it is a little scary, especially if it is me and Beth, not so much Keisha, but they see the questions we ask as being what we really care about, because it is 'eye-to-eye' and so that is what gets followed up on. And we don't ask about safety, or anything relating to safety like ergonomics. We only ask questions about performance."

Keisha nodded. "I didn't hear that, but I did hear that the KPI review meetings are seen as a meaningless exercise."

Beth stood up and wrote on the whiteboard. "Hypothesis Validated. Managers care more about KPIs than safety."

Keisha stood up and took the pen from Beth. She wrote. "Observation: Our KPI review meetings are seen as a meaningless exercise."

She sat down again. "Okay, so now what do we do?"

Roberta spoke first. "I think we need to create some leader standard work[2] around the questions we're asking in the warehouse, so that we start to emphasize safety. That is a PDCA cycle right there, planning what we going to do and trying it out, and seeing if it makes a difference. We also need to do something about those meetings! I also want to go back and look at our hypothesis about trust. Keisha, I'd like you to do an A3 on that, since you supervise the warehouse. Beth, you can be her A3 coach."

"I thought lean was supposed to make our lives easier," said Keisha, only half-joking.

"It will be easier when the warehouse is a safe place to work," replied Roberta.

PRACTICE THIS TODAY

If you're practicing PDCA, how much time are you spending on "Plan" proportional to the other steps? Are you thinking of hypotheses to test? How much time are you spending on the "Check" step? Are you tempted to move quickly to "Act?" How might you take a more scientific approach to your PDCA cycles?

Notes

1. The "Five Whys" is a method to find the root cause of a problem by asking "why" iteratively. It is attributed to Sakichi Toyoda. A related CPS tool that opens thinking to changing current conditions is the "Why/Why Not Chain." In this approach, the questions "why?" and "why not" are alternated.
2. Leader standard work consists of planned routines for lean leaders to ensure that they visit the *gemba,* and support employees by asking good questions, listening, and coaching.

Chapter 13

Solving the Trust Issue in the Warehouse

A week later, Keisha sat down with Beth to review her A3. Linda was also in the room. As Beth's coach, she was going to coach Beth later on how Beth had coached Keisha. After a few minutes, Beth and Keisha almost forgot that Linda was there.

"Thank you for sharing your A3 with me," said Beth, "I really appreciate you getting it to me earlier so I could thoroughly read it and think about my questions. Would you like to walk me through your updates, and I'll share my questions?"

Keisha nodded. "I have been working on the analysis. I have mostly been interviewing people in the warehouse. If you look at my fishbone diagram, I'm looking at six areas: people, materials, measurements, culture, management, and equipment. I've put nuggets from my interviews into most of these categories."

"I see," said Beth. "How did you pick those categories?"

"I learned that the fishbones usually have six categories, but they didn't all seem to fit our problem. This isn't a problem with a physical product. One category I changed was 'methods,' because we don't really have a process for sharing problems to document."

Keisha stopped and looked at Beth. "Oh, my goodness. What did I just say?"

"We have no process for sharing problems. So, no methods section on your fishbone."

"Oh boy. That is pretty revealing, isn't it?"

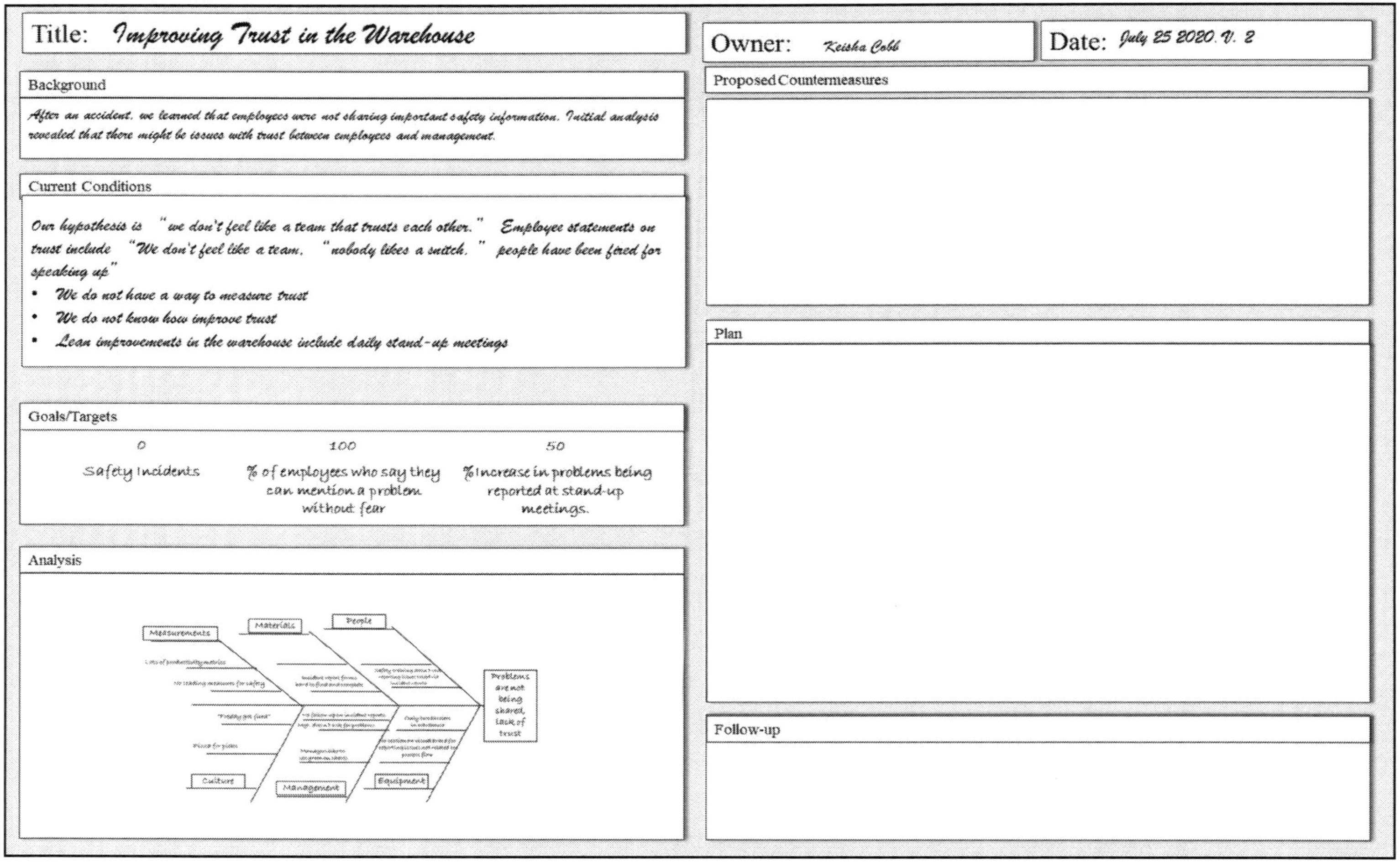
Title: Improving Trust in the Warehouse
Owner: Keisha Cobb
Date: July 25 2020. V. 2
Background
After an accident, we learned that employees were not sharing important safety information. Initial analysis revealed that there might be issues with trust between employees and management.
Current Conditions
Our hypothesis is "we don't feel like a team that trusts each other." Employee statements on trust include "We don't feel like a team, "nobody likes a snitch." people have been fired for speaking up"
We do not have a way to measure trust
We do not know how improve trust
Lean improvements in the warehouse include daily stand-up meetings
Goals/Targets
0
Safety Incidents
100
% of employees who say they can mention a problem without fear
50
% increase in problems being reported at stand-up meetings.
Analysis
Measurements
Materials
People
Culture
Management
Equipment
Problems are not being shared, lack of trust
Proposed Countermeasures
Plan
Follow-up

Figure 13.1 Keisha's A3.

Beth opened her mouth to say something, then remembered she was coaching, not managing. She paused for a moment. "So, Keisha, what do you plan to do?"

"Add a methods section to my little fish skeleton here. For sure. But let me show you what I added. 'Management' and 'Culture.'"

"How are you defining 'culture?'"

"I heard someone say that culture was the stories we tell each other so I put the story about someone getting fired for bringing up a problem in that section, and I also heard a lot about how important 'pizza for picks' is to people."

"Tell me more," said Beth. She remembered something about "pizza for picks" being initiated as a reward program.

"'Pizza for picks' was a monthly award. Whoever had the best pick rate for the month would get a gift certificate for a family-size pizza. We haven't done it for almost a year, but people in the warehouse really liked it. And because it was an award for individuals, it kind of created a competition between people."

"Interesting," Beth remarked. "How do you see that being pertinent to trust in the warehouse?"

"I think being competitive made people not want to help each other or share information."

Once again, Beth was about to say something, and changed her mind. She decided to ask a question to drive Keisha to think divergently. "What are all the ways you could check that out?"

"Oh, let me think about that." Keisha made a note on her A3 in the "Plan" section.

"How can you include this idea about the contest causing a competitive spirit on the A3? I don't see it here yet."

"You're right, that should be in the analysis section." She made another note.

"Tell me about 'Freddy got fired.'"

"That is related to something we heard when did our Five Whys interviewing. A couple of people told me that a certain employee got fired for reporting a safety situation. I had to go back and look at this employee's file because this happened before I started working here. He was dismissed for cause, but it was after several months of tardiness and absentee issues. He had been on a performance improvement plan, but he continued to have attendance problems. There were some other performance issues as well."

"What did the people you talked to think happened?"

"The funny thing is, none of them knew this employee. He was terminated before they started too. They said they were told that he was always in trouble for complaining about safety issues, and that was why he was put on a PIP and eventually fired."

Beth sighed. She was struggling to ask questions, and not make a statement. "What are all the reasons you can think of to explain why this story is being told?"

"It's a good story. We don't have stories to tell about how someone was rewarded for sharing a problem. Somebody is enjoying telling this story. Hmm … I will need to think of some more reasons – and some ways to check them out."

Beth finally allowed herself to make a statement. "I feel like we're getting somewhere important with your exploration into 'culture' and 'management.' Have you considered having someone interview you on why you didn't tell me about changing the pick rate? Or at least reflecting on that yourself?"

Keisha looked shocked. "No. I mean, I could. And we might want to interview you, too. Or ask you to do your own reflection."

Beth felt a sting of conscience. "You're right. I need to examine my own behavior. I guess thinking divergently means I need to include myself and my behavior among the possible reasons for the lack of trust."

Linda spoke up – Beth and Keisha had almost forgotten she was in the room.

"Now you're getting to the real heart of lean." She stood up on write on the whiteboard.

> "Lean": A socio-technical system for developing and managing people in organizations so that they can solve problems and continuously improve the organization to deliver value to customers.

Linda circled two words in the definition: "developing" and "people." She sat down again. Beth and Keisha stared at the board.

"I think I understand," said Beth, softly. "Solving this problem is not only about safety in the warehouse. It is about Keisha and me becoming better leaders for our employees. We're the ones being developed to be better managers and leaders."

Keisha stood up and picked up a red marker. She went to the board and underlined the word "socio-technical."

"Yeah," she said. "I didn't understand that word." She circled "socio." "How can our employees have trust, if I don't even trust Beth?"

Beth looked at Keisha, shocked. "What do you mean?" She had been wondering why Keisha hadn't told her about the change in the pick rate, ever since she had heard about it.

Linda spoke up again. "I think the coaching session is over. Good job, Beth. You did well as a coach. But now you and Keisha need a different kind of conversation, one that should probably not include me."

Beth watched Linda leave the room. There was an uncomfortable silence. Keisha sat down at the table and stared at her hands. Beth thought about all the time they had spent together, all the work they had done together, all the happy hours, and holiday parties. She had never given Keisha a bad performance review.

"Okay," Beth thought to herself. "What question do I ask?" She imagined what Carlo might say. A question that invites a divergent set of answers?

"Keisha. In what ways am I not trustworthy?"

She was trying to sound calm, but her heart was beating as fast as if she had just climbed three flights of stairs. Her palms were clammy.

"Well, I didn't say you weren't trustworthy. I said I don't trust you. But okay …"

"Do you want some sticky notes?"

Keisha laughed. "No, that's fine. I don't need sticky notes. I guess, you're very hard driving sometimes. A lot of the time. Once you come up with something, we all need to get on board and go with your program. And once you get going on something, you're not good at listening to other people's input."

"Can you give me an example?"

"All of this lean stuff we've been doing in the warehouse. You heard about supermarkets from Linda, or in training or something, and you were determined to set one up in the warehouse. It was like a shiny object, and you went for it, and we all had to get on board."

"It's working, isn't it? Doesn't it improve the picking for common parts?"

"That's not the problem. It's a good idea, it works. It's not the supermarket, it's that once you heard that idea, you didn't want to listen to any other ideas. I tried to talk to you about the pick rate once, but you told me to wait. So, I just went ahead and changed it, and kind of hoped you'd be happy when you found out, and not mad. You know what they say: ask forgiveness, not permission."

"You thought I'd be mad? It's not like I walk around yelling at people."

"No, you don't yell. But you can be intimidating when you're passionate about something. You're articulate, you present good arguments, and you make good points. You don't make space for other people. That's why people don't tell you things. It's not that they don't want to get yelled at. They just don't want to get in the way of Beth when she's on a roll."

"Wow. Thank you. That took some courage." Beth thought about her own relationship with Roberta. She wondered if she was modelling some of Roberta's impatience with her own team. "I need to reflect on that."

"Beth, you're a nice person. And you have been a good boss. But if this lean stuff is going to stick, don't we all need to change?"

Beth nodded her head. "Linda has been saying that. And Carlo too, I believe. I didn't know what they meant though. It's not about being nice, is it?"

"Being nice? I don't think so. It is about being more demanding. More demanding of good thinking. Not stopping with the first idea. Having us all think harder, more deeply. Having the courage to share ideas, having the will to listen to them."

Beth added, "Having the courage to listen to bad news, having the will to tackle the problem, not the person reporting it." She paused for a moment. "You know, if I had really listened to you about the pick rate, I probably would have just told you it was a bad idea. But I could have done three other things, instead. I could have thought about 'Praise First,' and come up with some good points about the idea to move my thinking away from

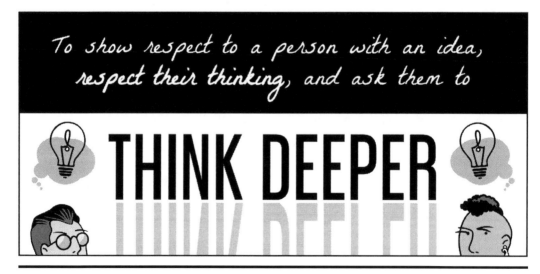

Figure 13.2 To Show Respect.

'fight or flight.' Perhaps I could have asked you to run an experiment with pick rate. Or I could have asked you to go and think deeper. Any of those responses would have indicated more respect for you than just telling you it was a bad idea."

"Which it probably was," said Keisha, a little sheepishly.

"I don't know. Maybe we should experiment with the pick rate." Beth looked at Keisha's A3. "What are you going to do with this?"

"I think I found a root cause. Now I'm going to see if I can come up with some countermeasures."

"Which are going to involve me, right?"

"And me," said Keisha.

PRACTICE THIS TODAY

How have you grown as a lean leader? What might you do to continue your growth? Where might you be holding your co-workers and employees back? What do you need to be free to lead?

Chapter 14

Creativity and the Improvement Kata

It was a rainy Monday when Beth next met with Linda to discuss her progress as a lean thinker. Although they usually met in the office, Beth had asked to meet at a coffee shop near her house, as she had to take Connor to a dentist appointment afterwards. They ordered their coffees and found a quiet corner. As usual, Linda asked Beth what her overall goal was in her path as lean leader. Instead of answering, Beth asked Linda a question. "Why do you always ask me that question?" Linda looked Beth in the eye. "Why do you think I always start with that question?" Beth laughed. "And you always answer my question with questions! Well, standards are important in lean, so I guess it is a standard way for us to start."

Linda took a sip of her coffee. "It is, but why that question? What might be the reason to start by reminding ourselves of your goal?"

"Because I need to recall where I am aiming to be as a lean thinker." Linda nodded her head. "Why is that?"

Beth laughed again. "Because, for me, especially, it is easy to get off track and lose focus on where I am headed."

Now it was it was Linda's turn to chuckle. "Fair enough. What is the next question I always ask?"

Beth paused to think for a moment. "I know! What is your target condition for this coaching cycle?"

Linda nodded her head again. "And the next question?"

"What is the current condition?" Beth had heard the questions so many times, she was ready with the next ones as well. "And then, what did you plan to do in the last week? And what was the result? What did you learn? And what is your next experiment? You always ask the same questions!"

Linda reached in her pocket and pulled out a dog-eared card and handed it to Beth.

IMPROVEMENT KATA

1. Understand the direction or challenge.
2. Grasp the current condition.
3. Establish the next target condition.
4. Experiment toward the next target condition.

"So, the questions you ask me take me through these steps. But what is a kata?"

"Okay, we will have a conversation about kata today. But we will get to those questions about your lean leadership growth before our coffee gets cold.

"In 2009, Mike Rother published the result of his research into the underlying thinking pattern at Toyota – he called this 'The Toyota Kata.' In martial arts, a 'kata' is a pattern that is practiced repeatedly, until it is encoded into muscle memory. Mike's thesis is that the thinking pattern of the 'improvement kata,' and an accompanying thinking pattern of a 'coaching kata' are encoded into Toyota's muscle memory. This means that every employee is always getting better and better at a scientific approach to problem solving. The improvement kata consists of the four steps on the card:

1. Understand the challenge (this is where you want to go and is usually a big lofty and hard to achieve goal).
2. Grasp the current condition (this is where you're now).
3. Set your next target condition (this is how far you want to go in the timeframe you have set).
4. Experiment toward your target condition.

"Let's use a real problem that you're facing right now as an example. The work in the warehouse?"

Beth thought about Keisha's A3 and the progress they were making on building trust. "That is really Keisha's work. I want to get back to the contact center. We have been so occupied with the warehouse that I haven't addressed those problems yet."

"What is the problem you're trying to solve?"

"What isn't the problem there?" Beth mused. "They are overworked, understaffed, not meeting customer needs ..."

She thought about it for a moment. "I think cross-training would make a big difference there. The staff get a lot of calls that need knowledge of the new customer app to solve, and a lot of them can't answer questions about the app."

"That sounds good," said Linda, "for an example. You would start with **1. Understanding the challenge**. Can you state it for me? – and write it in your notebook."

Beth thought for a moment. "It would be great if all the contact center staff could respond to every type of customer inquiry so that customers get all the services they are seeking in one call with one representative."

Linda didn't look very happy, but she said, "Okay we can use that as a place to start. Now you need to: **2. Grasp the current condition**."

This felt easy for Beth, as she had been thinking about this problem a lot. "I know that no employee is trained to answer all types of inquiries, especially the app questions; I do know that if someone calls with a question that can only be answered by one person, they may wait days to get an answer. Also, something we don't know is the types of calls we get each day. We do know that a lot of calls are being abandoned before they are resolved."

Linda nodded. "Write that in your notebook. and then you will **3. Set the next target condition**."

Beth paused. "Isn't that the goal?"

"Do you think you can achieve your goal by tomorrow? Think about the warehouse. What did you learn there?"

"We're going to be working on that for a long time. Building trust doesn't happen overnight. And the contact center issues have been going on for months, so they won't be solved by tomorrow. But why tomorrow?"

"One of the benefits of the improvement kata is that it keeps your learning cycles small. It doesn't have to be tomorrow, but it should be soon. When you talked about the current condition, you mentioned several obstacles. Do they help you think about your next target condition?"

"Okay, so we need to know what type of inquiries we get. That will take a little time to track, but I can make a tracking sheet for the contact center folks to fill out."

"Hold on!" said Linda, "Let's write down the target condition first."

Beth scribbled in her notebook, and after writing and crossing out a few sentences she said, "By next Monday, be able to track incoming requests."

Linda nodded. "Now we can talk about how you're going to

4. experiment toward that target condition."

"I can set up an easy tracking system so we can track the inquiries for the next week or so. Experiment – that means I will run this like a PDCA cycle, right?"

"Right! And how soon do you think you can show me the results of your experiment?"

"We meet again on Wednesday. How would that be?"

"Wednesday would be good. Are you really going to do this? This was intended to be an example, to explain the improvement kata to you."

"I have to solve this problem, and can't we build this into our coaching sessions?"

"This is a good way for you to develop your skills as a lean leader. But tell me what else you learned in the warehouse."

Beth smiled ruefully. "I almost did it again. I am so excited by what you just taught me that I was ready to run off and foist this on the contact center staff. My leadership is not about what I do, or what I think is right. It is about how the people who report to me are learning, so they can make improvements. My goal is: *'It would be great if I were a lean leader who created trust so that her employees and supervisors could see and solve problems.'*"

"Which means what?"

"I need to meet with Mo and find out what he is thinking first."

"What does that mean for the goal for improvement in the contact center?"

"We're going to have to work together to determine and set the goal. But I like the idea of the kata for the contact center. I can't see them doing A3s. Well, maybe Mo can do an A3 or two ..."

Linda nodded. "With the kata we can make a visual board, which we call a story board, that will work kind of like an A3. And Mo might need an A3 or more than one A3 for the larger problem. When are you going to have that meeting with Mo?"

"I will set it up for tomorrow. Can you coach me to coach Mo on the kata?"

"Yes, I can.

"Of course, I will be asking you those questions I always ask.

1. What is the goal?
2. What is your target condition?
3. Where are you now?
4. What did you plan to try in your last step?
5. What was the result?
6. What did you learn?
7. What is your next experiment?

"This coaching interaction would be guiding you to deeper thinking about the challenge you're working on. It would also help to encode the improvement kata into your mental muscle memory."

"Let me guess," Beth responded. "There is a book on this I should read."

"There is more than one book on the improvement kata, and I will send you some titles in my follow-up email. But for now, let's get back to today's questions and work on building your muscle memory for this pattern!"

After the meeting, Beth pondered this discussion. She was very excited about finally getting to work on the nagging contact center issue, but she wondered how her learning on creativity would align with her new knowledge of the improvement kata. The next morning, she called Carlo. She got right to the point.

"Carlo, have you ever heard of the improvement kata?"

"I have. It is an interesting way of making sure that you don't get stuck in solution-based thinking, and for making small progress that adds up to big changes."

"But how does it work with creativity principles? Does it work with creativity principles?

She could hear Carlo taking a deep breath. "Well, I haven't really thought that through. But I would love to think it through with you."

Beth told him about the problem that she and Linda had discussed, the issues in the contact center, starting with the example goal. She had written it out in her notebook. Even though she and Linda had agreed she needed to meet with Mo before proposing any goals, she had already tried to put together a tracking sheet. Then she thought better of it, after she imagined what would happen if she had tried to get the contact center associates to use the tracking sheet. She sent Carlo a picture of the notebook page so he could follow along.

What is the goal?	It would be great if all the contact center staff could respond to every type of customer inquiry so that customers get all the services they are seeking in one call with one representative
Where are you now? (Current condition)	No employee is trained to answer all types of inquiries. We don't know if and how inquiries vary day to day
What is the target condition?	Know how many inquiries we get, and what type
What did you try to do in your last step?	By tomorrow, set up an easy tracking system so we can track the inquiries for the next week or so
What was the result?	The team didn't think the tracking tool I came up with was easy to use
What did you learn?	I need to get the team's input to design a good tracking tool
What is your next experiment?	Sit with a team member to see what points in the process might be easy to track

Carlo listened carefully and then asked: "What are all the ways that creativity could be injected into this process to make it more effective?"

Beth laughed. "What is it with you coaches and asking questions?"

Carlo let that one pass. "Beth, I believe that creativity is vital in each step of the improvement kata. Let's start with the 'goal.' First, we need to recognize that in the improvement kata, the goal is often something handed down from higher in the organization – but where does this goal come from?"

"It comes from me, the associate director. So, yes, it is handed down from management!"

"How did you state the goal?"

"I stated the goal as: 'It would be great if all the contact center staff could respond to every type of customer inquiry so that customers get all the services they are seeking in one call with one representative.'"

Carlo didn't answer for a moment.

"You still there?" Beth asked.

"Beth, is that a goal?"

"I think so. We want customers to get all the services they are seeking on the first call to the contact center."

Beth looked at the goal statement again. "I see why you're asking though. There is a solution built into that goal – that cross-training is the answer. By stating the goal in that way, I've already mentally eliminated some creative solutions. I fell into the solution trap again! I haven't really understood and

Figure 14.1   Deep Thinking.

clarified the goal. And as a leader, it's not a good idea for me to try to enroll my employees in going after a goal that hasn't been clarified. And as I realized yesterday, it isn't the best thing for me to set a goal that they haven't had input to."

Beth thought about her meeting with Linda yesterday. It was going to be harder than she had thought to change her habit of jumping in and trying to solve every problem herself.

"I converged too quickly on a goal. You know, Linda gave me a funny look when I stated the goal, but she was only thinking of it as an example, so she didn't ask me to think more deeply."

Carlo wanted to be reassuring. "Remember that your CPS tools can always be relied on to take you in the direction of deeper thinking. And deeper thinking is creative thinking."

"Carlo, do you agree that I'd better clarify the challenge before I get going with an improvement kata? What if I started with a question? What are all the ways that we might ensure customers get the services they need?"

"There you go," said Carlo, "this is an opportunity for divergent thinking. Exploring this question could result in a better outcome than jumping on the assumption that the solution must rest with the cross-training."

"So, I would create a set of options around this question, and then use convergent thinking to select the goals to work towards."

Beth heard Carlo clear his throat, but he didn't say anything.

She realized she had done it again. "I could engage the contact center employees as well. I already have a meeting set up with Mo this afternoon. But the folks in the contact center ..."

"They might have some ideas for you."

Beth sighed. "All of this takes time."

"And what if you don't spend that time? Do you have time to chase after the wrong goal or a poorly stated goal?"

"No," said Beth. "No time for that."

> ## PRACTICE THIS TODAY
>
> *Are you using the improvement kata? Think about how your goals/ challenges are set. What is the value of taking the time to ensure your goals are well-thought through?*

Chapter 15

Goal Setting in the Contact Center

Mo and Beth met in the hallway outside the contact center bullpen the next afternoon.

"How're things going?" Beth asked. She noticed that Mo didn't have his usual smile.

"They haven't improved," he answered. "And today I got this." He handed her a printed-out email.

Beth scanned it quickly. "Julie resigned?"

"I wasn't surprised. She was showing signs of getting ready to leave. It's been hard on her. She has been such a mainstay of the group, but that means she has had to pick up a lot of extra hours to cover for other people's absenteeism. Our sick days are completely out of control."

"Mo, I'm really sorry. I haven't been the support you need."

"Beth, I understand, I know what happened in the warehouse. I'm hoping this meeting today means you have some time for us now."

"Things are improving in the warehouse, and I've learned a lot. I keep thinking back to that day I spent here and what I saw, and frankly, what I didn't know how to see."

Mo looked at her quizzically. "I don't know what you mean. I'm guessing you're not here to tell me that there is more funding for headcount."

Beth laughed. "I wish! But no."

"So how are you going to help us?"

"I'm not. At least not directly. You and your team are going to learn to help yourselves. With my support, and Roberta's." Beth walked over to the contact center door. "Let's go in."

Because it was late afternoon, the contact center was relatively quiet. Only the customers on the West Coast, which was their smallest territory, were likely to call this late in the day.

"Mo, could you give me a tour? Pretend I've never been here before."

"Okay. If that is what you want."

"That's what I want."

"In that case, welcome to the contact center."

"What do you do here?"

"We answer the phone," Mo said, with the first grin she had seen since she arrived.

"No, seriously, Mo, what do you do here?"

"You mean like a mission statement? I can't remember it off the top of my head. Something something something, happy customers, something something."

"Mo."

"What do we do here? I guess, we try to solve customer problems. And most of the time we do solve those problems. And sometimes we can't, and we do a lot of apologizing because somebody else here in the company or one of our suppliers or the app developers screwed up."

"I hear you saying you solve customer problems and you apologize."

Mo rubbed his chin. "That's pretty much it. And I spend a lot of time on contact center analytics, but I am not sure anybody uses the analyses I do. If I don't do the reporting though, I get nasty emails from Quality Control."

"That doesn't sound like fun. I do look at the reports that you create, and I am hoping to use those analytics more as we work on solving your problems. Is Quality Control still listening to recordings of your calls?"

Mo sighed. "That is probably one of the reasons Julie left. QC sends people these little report cards, and they are not very encouraging. If, for example, a customer is so angry about an issue with the app that they hang up, that results in a negative rating on the QC feedback."

Beth remembered the call she had listened into, and Julie's calm and reassuring tone. That customer interaction probably earned Julie a poor rating. She made a mental note to include someone from QC in the improvement work in the contact center.

"Hey, Mo, what's going on with the visual display?" The large screen was dark.

"We realized that it wasn't helping us. So, I turned it off." Mo looked chagrined. "I know it was expensive and, heck, we asked for it. Maybe we can figure out a better way to use it."

"Mo, it is very important that the improvement work we're going to start here in the contact center is owned by you and the team. And to do it, we need to be clear on the goal we're headed for and how it links with the company goals. What would it take to get a group together to clarify a goal?"

"That will be tough. But maybe we can start with a meeting after first shift is over. I can persuade some folks to stay for a meeting, if they will get paid and probably fed."

"I can approve the overtime and get snacks. Let's look at calendars and see how soon we can get started."

Beth was happy and a little surprised to learn that the contact center associates were excited about getting started on improvements. It was only a few days before a small group of contact center folks, a woman from Quality Control, Mo, and Beth met in the cafeteria after first shift to get started. Linda and Carlo were there to facilitate.

Linda kicked off the meeting with an explanation of the improvement kata. She had brought brightly colored jigsaw puzzles with her for an exercise called "Kata in the Classroom."[1] She divided the group into two teams, explained the challenge (to complete the puzzle in 15 seconds) and invited each team to select a target condition for today (one team chose 45 seconds and the other team chose 52 seconds). In less than 10 minutes, the teams were competing intensely to reduce the length of time it took for them to assemble the puzzles. After each round, they asked themselves the coaching kata questions:

■ What is the target condition?
■ What did you try to do in your last step?
■ What was the result?
■ What did you learn?
■ What is your next experiment?

After four rounds, Linda called time, much to everyone's disappointment. Neither team had reached their target condition, but they were getting close.

"What was your biggest learning from this exercise?" asked Linda.

Mo raised his hand. "That little kid puzzles are harder than they look!" Everyone laughed. "No, seriously, that you need to experiment your way to achieving a challenge or even a target condition."

"Great insight," said Linda. "What else?"

"That different people have different skills and ideas." That was the woman from Quality Control, Carmen.

"Nice," said Linda. "What else?"

Geoff from the contact center raised his hand. "That it is good to have an approach, a method for improvement. We didn't agree what we should try at first but knowing that we had a way to try was helpful." He looked directly at Beth. "But I have a question. I feel like we don't know what our challenge is in the contact center. And because we don't know our challenge, we can't set a target condition."

Carlo stood up. "That's a perfect segue for what we're going to do next, which is to work on clarifying that challenge for the contact center. Thank you, Geoff." As Linda collected the puzzles, Carlo distributed materials to each participant.

Beth was expecting the usual stacks of sticky notes, but today Carlo had a stack of 8.5 × 11 sheets of paper.[2] Each one had rows of sticky notes, nine on each sheet. Beth did the math in her head. So, nine participants, if Linda and herself were included, times nine sticky notes per sheet, meant 81 stickies. Eighty-one ideas. She shook her head. That was going to require a lot of convergent thinking to manage.

Figure 15.1   Brainwriting Sheet.

Carlo was standing next to a flip chart. "Geoff was very accurate with what he said. This group needs to understand its challenge before undertaking improvement work. So today, we're going to work on that. Does everyone have a sheet in front of them? And a black marker?"

Carlo wrote a phrase on a flipchart sheet. "It would be great if …"

"Think about the contact center. What are your wishes and desires for the contact center? Write down three wishes or desires on the top row of your sheet of paper. For each one, start it with this phrase: 'It would be great if.' "

"Only three?" Beth asked.

"After you have written three, pass the sheet to the person to your right. You can keep writing your own wishes and desires or look at what is already on the sheet and see if it inspires other thoughts for you, or if you want to build on to or expand something you see."

"Can we write whatever we want?" someone asked.

"As long as it starts with 'It would be great if.' You can abbreviate it to 'IWBGI' if you don't want to write it out. I know I haven't explained divergent thinking and convergent thinking to this group yet, so let's take a moment to review the guidelines for divergent thinking."

Carlo asked Beth to provide an explanation for each of the guidelines, and she felt pleased that she was able to do so.

- Defer Judgment
- Combine and Build
- Seek Wild Ideas
- Go for Quantity.

The room was quiet for a while as people wrote and passed the papers around. The sheets filled up quickly and Carlo placed more on the table. After a while the energy seemed to ebb. Carlo said, "We find when we force a connection between something unrelated to the problem that it spurs ideas." Carlo pulled a picture from his stack of papers – it was a photograph of a forest in full leaf. "Think about this beautiful forest and its attributes – when you force a mental connection between this forest and the problem we're trying to solve in the contact center, what desires and wishes does that suggest?" Later he brought out a picture of an orchestra, and said, "Think of an orchestra. What are the attributes of an orchestra? Connect those attributes with the contact center. What does that bring to mind?"[3]

Carlo handed out even more sheets with sticky notes on them.

As people put their black markers down, some sat back from the table, Carlo asked them to take the completed sheets and place any stickies that related to the five company goals on flipchart sheets labeled with the goals.

- No safety incidents.
- Improve employee engagement by 50 percent.
- Improve net promoter score to 80.
- Bring 5 innovative new offerings to market.
- Increase operating margin to 10 percent.

In a few minutes, everyone had finished writing and most of the stickies were attached to a goal. Carlo needed to add two flipchart sheets to the employee engagement goal.

After a flurry of activity at the flipchart sheets, there were seven sticky notes that hadn't been added to the goal flipcharts.

> It would be great if we could stop doing reports no one reads.
> It would be great if we had magic wands.
> It would be great if there were no contact center.
> It would be great if the contact center ran the company.
> It would be great if we could see exactly what inventory is in the warehouse.
> It would be great if we killed the ordering app.
> It would be great if we could go out with a customer and see what they do all day.

"Right," said Carlo, "We should start by looking at these."

"I don't think so," Beth replied. "These are probably leftovers for good reason." She realized everyone was staring at her. "Look, we're not going to get magic wands, and this is about saving the contact center, not eliminating it."

"You know what," said Linda, catching Carlo's eye. "I could use a bio break. How about everyone else?"

"Sounds like a great idea," Carlo replied. He looked at the clock on the wall. "Ten minutes everyone?"

As the group left the cafeteria, Carlo steered Beth toward the windows. Outside the sun was setting and she realized the increasing darkness matched her mood.

"Beth, what's going on?" Carlo said gently. Beth noticed that Linda had come back into the cafeteria and Carlo motioned her to join them.

"I saw those stickies and I don't know, I just felt that a couple of them are out of line. Especially the one about eliminating the contact center. I know that is the thing that makes the most economic sense. We could outsource it, and that would be a boon to the bottom line. But I think it is important to have a US-based contact center and I know these people. I don't want them to lose their jobs. I really don't want to go there with this group. I am guessing the woman from QC wrote that."

"Do you know that?" asked Linda.

"No," Beth admitted.

Linda continued. "Beth, what did you feel, physically, when you saw that statement?"

"What do you mean?"

"What did your body tell you? What emotions did you experience?"

"I felt anxious, angry. My heart was beating faster. It was like my stomach lurched, frankly."

"Oh," said Carlo. "Could you have been in fight or flight mode?"

Beth smiled ruefully. "I guess I was. I guess I wasn't thinking with my frontal lobes."

"What was the impact on the rest of the group?" asked Linda.

"I'm the boss … so I guess I probably impacted how they felt about their ideas. I made somebody think their ideas were bad."

"And?" queried Linda.

"And I made it unsafe for people to bring up radical and possibly innovative ideas."

"Could be," said Carlo. "But it is not too late. You have a chance right now to amend what you said. What are you going to do?"

Beth looked at the setting sun. "I'm going to be honest with them about what just happened. And I'm going to listen to what that statement means to the person who wrote it."

"Do you need a moment?"

"No, I'm fine. Thanks for the questions."

Linda put her hand on Beth's arm. "Beth, do you remember when we first met, and I talked about lean thinking requiring a change in mindset? I believe you're well on your way to that change in mindset. But it is not visible to your employees yet."

As everyone gathered around again, Carlo addressed the group. "Beth has something she wants to share with you all."

Beth took a deep breath. "Hey, everyone, I need to share an insight that I just had. First, I want you to know that I care a lot about all of you, and the work of the contact center, and your well-being and success. So, when I saw those statements, I reacted hard. My insight is that even though I know I'm supposed to be encouraging innovation and risk-taking, I'm not good yet at listening and asking questions before I make judgments. I need more practice, and I want you to know that you can say anything to me. I want to hear it all, even if it is something, I don't like at first glance. I will be working on doing better and I hope you will help me." A couple of people murmured something and then there was a smattering of applause, led by Mo.

Carlo smiled. "Thanks, Beth. That was well said. I take it we can go ahead and look at these statements now?"

"Yes please!"

Carlo picked up the sticky with the statement "It would be great if there were no contact center." "Is the person who wrote this willing to speak about it?"

Everyone was silent. Some people were looking at their feet, while others looked around the group to see if anyone would confess to owning that sticky note.

"It's perfectly safe to do so!" added Beth.

Mo raised his hand. "That was me. And it does require some explanation. Believe it or not, I wrote this one too." He pointed to "It would be great if the contact center ran the company."

Somebody laughed, breaking the tension in the room. "One of these things is the opposite of the other!"

Mo nodded. "What I mean is that what we're doing most of right now is addressing problems that are caused by other departments and the fact that the app doesn't work. We solve problems for customers and then the next day, the same problems happen again. All of that should be unnecessary, meaning that we shouldn't need a contact center, at least not one that does what we're doing most of the time. At the same time, we're talking to customers a lot, and we learn a lot about their needs, but we're not considered to be as smart as the people in marketing who supposedly own the customer experience. If we ran the company, the company would know a lot more about the customer experience."

Geoff spoke up. "He is so right. And I need my job, but this isn't the job I need, if you know what I mean." Others in the group nodded their heads in agreement.

"Carlo?" said Beth. "Do you have some of those dots you like to use to show the favored ones?"

"Do I have dots? Of course, I have dots."

Beth looked at the guidelines for convergent thinking posted on the wall.

- Be Deliberate
- Check Your Objectives
- Improve Your ideas
- Be Affirmative
- Consider Novelty.

"I'm going to be deliberate, and I'm thinking about our objectives, which include improving our net promoter score and increasing employee engagement, and therefore, considering the novelty of these two statements, I want to give each one a beautiful dot."

She looked at the other participants. A couple looked puzzled, but most were smiling.

"We will get to the dots in a minute," said Carlo. Beth had a moment of self-recrimination. "I did it again," she thought. "I didn't trust the process, or my people."

Carlo continued. "Mo, please think about these two statements. Do you want to reword them?"

"I think I do. 'It would be great if the contact center solved company problems permanently.' And 'It would be great if the contact center led the customer conversation.'"

"Are they aligned with the company objectives?"

"Yes, they are." Mo moved the rewritten statements to the 'Net Promoter Score" flipchart. "They both could lead to customers recommending us to others, because their experience with the contact center is so fantastic, and the company could respond better to their needs."

Carlo looked at the clock. "Folks, we're at the end of our planned time together. We're going to have to do some more work to get to a small group of challenges for your improvement kata. Are you willing to come back and do the work?"

Geoff looked at Beth and Mo. "If we do this, will Roberta and Brandon go along with what we come up with?"

Beth nodded. "If we can articulate how it benefits the business, I don't see why not."

"Then I'm in. Let's pick a time."

"Thanks, Geoff!" Mo replied. "See, Beth, this is the best team in the company."

After the session, Beth walked out of the building into the dark parking lot with Linda and Carlo.

"How do you feel now?" Linda asked.

"I'm good." Beth smiled. "I should be terrified, because I think we're going to create a big ruckus. But I'm feeling very positive about this team and what they might do. I just have to get Roberta and Brandon on board."

Linda and Carlo spoke simultaneously. "Let's talk about that!"

"Tomorrow," Beth replied. "I'm going home to see my kid."

PRACTICE THIS TODAY

What might you do to make sure that the most novel solutions get appropriate consideration?

Notes

1. You can get instructions and materials for Kata in the Classroom at: www. katatogrow.com/instructor-materials.
2. This tool for group brainstorming is called 'brainwriting." See Appendix 2.
3. Carlo used a tool for divergent thinking called "forced connections." Read about it in Appendix 2.

Chapter 16

Gaining Acceptance

Beth and Mo met in the hallway outside the meeting room where Brandon and the directors were holding their monthly business review meeting. Mo was wearing a tie and a dress shirt. He looked nervous and paced the small space.

"Mo, are you okay?" asked Beth.

Mo made a scoffing sound. "My whole career and the future of my team hang on the success of this presentation. So, I'm doing just fine!"

"I'm here to support you. And Roberta is too. And you're very well prepared. You have done a good job preparing the ground for the idea of transforming the contact center into a customer experience center with strong connections to sales, marketing, and the strategic direction of GPS."

"Preparing the ground." This was a term that Beth and Mo had learned from Linda. She had used a Japanese word, "*nemawashi*," and had explained that it literally meant to prepare a plant for transplantation by "going around the roots." In business practice, it meant to get stakeholders on board with a new proposal by informally sharing it with them and getting their feedback. Linda and Beth had supported Mo and his team in developing a proposal A3, which Mo had shared with almost all the directors individually in preparation for this meeting.

Carlo had added his perspective from CPS. "It does you no good to have the best ideas or solutions in the world, if you can't get people to accept them. Planning for implementation starts with identifying the path to acceptance. And this might require further cycles of divergent and convergent thinking. You need to identify the people and other factors that will assist in implementation, and, just as importantly, identify the people and factors that will resist or hold back implementation."

Mo had used this advice. He, Beth, Roberta, and several members of the contact center team had brainstormed on assisters and resisters. He paid special attention to directors who might support the change, but just as much attention to those who might resist. Several times, when a director had an objection to a component of the proposal, Mo had rephrased their objection as a question: "How might we ...?" Springboarded by the question, the director and Mo were able to develop options to address the concern. The A3 he was about to take into the director's meeting was enriched by the creativity of the directors themselves.

Brandon opened the door and invited them into the conference room. "Hey there, Beth and Mo. It's great to have you join us today. We have been looking forward to this part of the meeting."

Beth and Mo took seats at the table. Beth sat next to Roberta, while Mo was given a seat next to Brandon. Mo passed around the updated copies of his A3 proposal. Beth noticed that each director had a stack of sticky notes in front of them, and black markers were strewn around the table. Someone waved at her from the side of the room, and she saw that Linda and Carlo were seated in chairs along the wall.

"I hope it is okay that Linda and Carlo are here," said Brandon. "They have been integral to this work, and I thought they might enjoy seeing some of the fruits of their labors."

"It's okay with me," said Mo.

"Likewise," Beth said in agreement.

"Mo, thank you for sharing your A3 with us before the meeting," said Brandon. "I know you have been working hard to get feedback and input from most of the directors. I'm going to let them ask you any final questions before we move forward. Was there anyone you didn't meet with?"

"Only Jeremy. I think I met with everyone else. Um, Brandon, do you want me to go over the A3?"

"Only if you have significant updates that we haven't seen."

"Not really. I added some ideas about communication after I met with you." Beth knew that Mo had been rehearsing what to say to the directors all week, so while this was a relief, it was also perhaps a let-down.

"Well, then, let's go around the table and hear what questions people have."

George Windrow, the marketing director, was first with a question. Beth knew that their proposal was very likely to step on marketing's toes, and George was known for his forceful personality.

"Thank you, Mo – and Beth – for sharing this very interesting proposal. Mo, you know that in marketing we want to really know the customers, and we work closely with Roberta's sales team to gain a lot of the information we need. The concern I raised with you was that we would be getting a flood of information that we wouldn't be able to make sense of, and I see here that you have some plans to manage that. The only question I have now is, how soon can you run some experiments to validate this approach?"

"Is tomorrow okay?"

"Tomorrow?" George sounded skeptical.

"Well, tomorrow we can give you a report of the suggestions for new product lines that customers have made over the past month." Mo paused. "There will be other reports, but this one is ready now."

"Any other questions, George?" asked Brandon.

"No, I'm good," said George. "Glad to see these guys stepping up to contribute."

Beth was about to defend Mo and the contact center but stopped when Roberta patted her hand. "George is trying to work in the new way," Roberta whispered. "He is a slow learner."

"Like me," Beth whispered in reply.

Roberta smiled. "Like all of us."

Sandy, the head of IT, spoke up next. "Mo, you know we have spent a huge amount of money on the GPS ordering app. You have proposed discontinuing most use of the app, and I see that proposal is still in here ..."

Carlo, still sitting quietly in the corner, happened to clear his throat.

"I am getting to a question," said Sandy. "Can you provide any data that will help us redesign the app, if and when funding is available?"

"We can provide you with data, Sandy," Mo replied. "We can also connect you with customers willing to continue to use the app and test future versions. Some customers are happy with it and want us to continue to move in a digital direction. But some customers are not going to be able to make that switch. That's why we want to work with sales and the marketing team to ensure that the customer experience is customized to the individual customer."

Roberta spoke up. "I don't have a question obviously, but I do want to say that I'm very pleased that the contact center is planning to work more closely with sales. Frankly, even though they have both been in my department for a long time, there hasn't been a lot of cross-fertilization."

Brandon looked around the room. "Any other questions?" He included Linda and Carlo in his gaze. "Linda, Carlo, any comments?"

Everyone shook their head. "Because this is such a big change, and has impacts far beyond Roberta's department, I'd like to hear from each one of you that you support and are committed to advancing this initiative. Carlo?"

Carlo stood up and drew a target on the whiteboard. Above the target he wrote "Create a Center for Customer Engagement."

"Would each of the directors, and you, Brandon, write your initials on a sticky note. Then come up here and place your sticky on the target. If you're 100 percent on board and willing to support Mo's proposal, place your sticky right in the center of the target. If you have concerns, or problems that need to be solved before you can commit, place your sticky on the appropriate ring of the target. We will discuss and address the concerns before we leave this meeting."

"Is that a threat?" ask Brandon. "It's getting pretty late in the day."

"It's really a promise," replied Carlo, "that we will work on this until all the directors can support the path forward. This is not about achieving consensus, and compromise, but about strengthening the proposal so that it can be implemented successfully, with full acceptance of the leaders of this company. The goal is to get everyone on the bullseye for full commitment."

"Well, we still have a lot to learn before full implementation," said Mo. "I don't think what we end up with will be exactly like the proposal on the A3."

"True," said Carlo, "and let's start that learning now." Beth watched as each director added their initialed sticky note to the target. Almost all were in the center. One was in the ring outside the center, and one was at the very edge of the target. Carlo picked that one up first. "Who is SN?" he asked. "Is that you, Sandy?"

"Yes, that's me." Sandy, the IT director, raised her hand.

"Is this about the app?" asked Carlo.

"No, it's not about the app," said Sandy. "I am disappointed about the app, after the dollars and the effort we put into it, but I'm not going to push it if the customers are not getting benefit from it. My issue with not being able to fully support this proposal is about the people in the contact center. These are not the highest-level people in the company, if I can put it delicately, and I'm not convinced they can take on the level of problem solving and analysis that this proposal requires."

Beth glanced at Mo. He didn't react.

"Let's phrase that as a question, Sandy," said Carlo. "In what ways …"

Sandy paused for a moment.

"In what ways might we support and educate the contact center associates to perform analytics and problem solving?"

Brandon looked at Sandy. "You have some pretty good analysts on your team. Maybe you could help?"

Mo spoke up. "We'd be happy to get the support and maybe even some training."

Carlo addressed Sandy. "If we could find ways to develop analytical skill in the current staff, would you be able to move your sticky note closer to the center?"

"I could move it. Not to the center but closer. Close enough to move forward."

"I will add training on analytical skills to the A3," said Mo. "What else?"

Sandy leaned forward, scrutinizing the A3 in front of her. "You may need to hire some different skill sets, Mo."

"I have some openings to fill. Can you help me with position descriptions?" Mo chuckled to himself. "No, wait a minute. How *might you* help me with position descriptions?"

Sandy shifted her attention from the A3 to the calendar on her phone. "I have time tomorrow to discuss that with you. How is 2 p.m.?"

"Sandy, where is your sticky now?" asked Carlo.

"Getting closer to the center," Sandy admitted. "Close enough for me to be on board."

"Show me where to put it," Carlo said, picking up the sticky note.

"Right on the innermost ring. Yeah, that's it." Sandy smiled. "If Mo and I can work together, that will be good."

"Which leaves us," said Carlo, "with this one." He picked up the other sticky note that was outside the center circle.

"That's mine." This was Jeremy Wong, the HR Director. Beth had been wondering when Jeremy would weigh in. "My concerns are like Sandy's. I don't believe this group can pull this off. They are just not the talent that can do that." He spoke directly to Brandon. "Brandon, we need to talk about this without Mo and Beth in the room."

Roberta spoke up. "We're committed to transparency here. I would like Mo and Beth to stay." Beth looked at Mo. His hands were shaking as he organized the materials in front of him at the table. Brandon nodded. "How about we give Mo a break, but Beth will stay. Mo, don't go too far, we'll need you back here in a few minutes."

Mo looked relieved as he stood up and left the room. Brandon turned back to Jeremy. "What is your issue? And please state it as a question inviting a creative response."

Jeremy glared at Brandon. "Brandon, I'm tired of this stuff. I would just like to say what needs to be said. What everyone in in the room is thinking but doesn't have the guts to say." He looked at Beth and Roberta. "Look, Mo is a nice guy. But he has run that contact center into the ground. He doesn't have an MBA – heck, I don't know if he even has a degree. The people in the contact center are mostly high school graduates. They are not capable of delivering this kind of a change, and Mo is not the kind of leader who can lead a change like that."

Roberta stood up. She was holding a copy of Mo's A3. "Jeremy, do you believe this is a strategic and valuable change?"

Jeremy nodded. "It's quite brilliant. Very strategic."

Roberta continued, an angry note in her voice. "Do you know who came up with this idea? It wasn't me. It wasn't Beth. It was Mo. And Mo and his team developed this proposal and strengthened the ideas in it. I have complete confidence in them. The question I would ask is, how might HR support Mo to continue to develop the leadership skills he needs for this change?" She sat down.

Carlo turned to Jeremy. "Jeremy, what would get you on board? You didn't place your sticky note all that far outside the center."

"I was going to say all that is needed is to replace Mo with a more qualified leader. I get the sense that is a non-starter."

Roberta started to speak, but Carlo interrupted. "Jeremy, may I rephrase that for you?"

Jeremy sighed. "Sure, go ahead."

"How might we ensure that the leadership of the contact center is ready and able to lead this change?"

"I agree," said Roberta. "I have no desire to put Mo into a position where he is set up to fail. But I think we can support him, and I also believe that with Beth's engagement and coaching, using the improvement kata and more A3s as needed, Mo will succeed. And if he doesn't, it will be our failure, not his."

Brandon turned to Jeremy. "Thank you for sharing your concern. I want you to know I heard it, and I understand what you're worried about. I appreciate the efforts you have been making to upgrade the talent in the company, and to hold us to high standards." He looked at Carlo. "Let's do some brainstorming on this question. Beth, please ask Mo to join us. I would like his input on what support he needs."

In the hallway, Beth quickly told Mo what had happened. Mo laughed out loud. "That is pretty funny! Jeremy said what I was thinking. I don't know if I can lead this change. I was more than half-expecting to end up being replaced."

"You were? That never crossed my mind."

"None of us are ready to lead this change. But we're all ready to learn how to lead change. And I think you have a head start on some people in that room."

They went back inside to find Jeremy moving his sticky note to the center of the target. "What happened?" asked Beth, a little afraid to hear the answer.

Jeremy looked chagrined. "I'm on board. It looks like I'm going to be Mo's leadership mentor. If he will have me."

"Great!" exclaimed Brandon. "Let's come up with some other ideas for supporting the leadership of this change."

By the end of the meeting, half a dozen strategies to support Mo and the contact center had been added to Mo's A3. Beth stayed to help Carlo pack up his supplies. Mo had gone ahead to report back to his team before they left for the day.

"Carlo, what was that you did with the target?" Beth asked.

"That is a CPS tool called 'targeting'. It is a convergence tool often used in planning for implementation. It works very well for gaining acceptance of an idea, and at the same time strengthening the idea. I also love it because it is so simple. Everyone understands a target. It does work best in the kind of culture that Brandon is building here. One where people are free, like Jeremy was, and Roberta was, to state their truth. Speaking of which, Beth, I didn't hear your voice much in this meeting. Why not? What was stopping you?"

"I know." Beth considered the reasons for that. "I know I can be 'intimidating' but I find all the directors together intimidating. And Roberta was speaking up very well for our group."

"I think you always have valuable things to say. Do me and Linda a favor. We won't be here forever. You're our legacy in a way. Speak up. Share what you know."

"I will," said Beth. "Thank you."

The next day, she went to HR and knocked on Jeremy's door. He looked up from his computer, surprised to see her. "Hi, Beth, what can I do for you?

"Hey Jeremy," she answered. "Do you have time this afternoon? I'd like to take you on a *gemba* walk of the contact center. I think you will learn a lot if you spend some time there."

PRACTICE THIS TODAY

What approaches and methods do you use to gain acceptance of new ideas? What might you do differently?

Chapter 17

Small Steps, Long Journey

Now that the contact center had a challenging goal, the team was eager to start using the improvement kata. Linda ran a few more sessions with jigsaw puzzles and handed out the cards with the questions to everyone. Mo and Beth and the people who had attended the first session, augmented by Erica, an associate from IT, as well as an associate from marketing, and one from sales, set up a meeting with Linda to write a handful of measurable objectives in support of the challenge of transforming into a customer experience center. Beth had asked Jeremy for a representative from HR and was astonished when Jeremy himself appeared in the doorway just as the meeting was ready to start.

Jeremy laughed when she questioned his presence. "Well, you know, HR is really only two people. I just assigned the least useful one to this meeting."

Beth sat in the corner. She had decided to simply observe this meeting and let Mo step into the group leadership role. She knew it would be an effort to keep her mouth shut, and she was determined to succeed.

Linda wrote the challenge on the whiteboard. "Create a Center for Customer Engagement."

"Mo, we've all read the A3, and many people here have contributed to it. But please tell us in your own words what it means to create a Center for Customer Engagement."

"For one thing, it means we're the center of the company. We interact with customers every day, we delight them, help them get their problems solved, and learn what they need and want. What we learn from customers drives the company strategy, directs which problems need to be solved in other departments, and provides valuable data to sales and to marketing."

"If you were to come in here tomorrow and you had magically achieved your goal overnight, how would you be able to tell?"

"Hmm, good question. I guess, the number of calls related to customer issues would be much less, a lot of the associates would be helping customers who don't want to use the app to easily order parts, we would be proactively reaching out to customers for input, and we would be spending more time on analytics and reporting, the reports we provide would be eagerly anticipated and used by the rest of the company for process improvement and better marketing and selling, we would spend proportionally less time on the phone. Oh, and call center associates would all be happy!"

Linda noted each of Mo's statements on the whiteboard. "Let's take these one at a time, starting with percentage of calls related to customer issues. What is the current data?"

"Last week, 87 percent of calls were due to customer issues, if you include problems with the app. If we only look at calls that aren't about app problems, 80 percent of those ones are customer issues like late deliveries, wrong part sent, etc."

"What are the rest of the calls?"

"We get a lot of requests for parts that we don't carry, about 15 percent of the non-app calls. And some calls we don't classify. Someone might call to compliment their delivery driver or to request a catalog or ask for instructions for a particular product."

"What would be a reasonable percentage of customer complaints?"

Mo laughed. "Zero, of course. But we don't have control over road traffic, or snowstorms in the Mid-West, for example, so a part might still be delivered late. Let's say, 10 percent. But if we can reduce the issues that lead to the calls, we will make a big difference in the volume of calls, so I'd rather have that as a measure."

The team decided that reduction of call volume related to issues or complaints to half of the current amount would permit time for the new activities they wanted to take on, including the analytics function, assisting the many customers who did not want to use the app, and proactively calling customers.

Linda showed them a visual board she had created on a mobile whiteboard. "This will be your kata story board for this challenge," she said, writing "Inbound Complaint Call Volume less than 500/day" in the upper right-hand corner.

"This will be a long journey," one of the team members sighed.

Focus Process: *Incoming Call Handling*		Challenge: *Inbound Complaint Call Volume less than 500/day Mo, Elizabeth and Erica*
Target Condition: Achieve By:	Current Condition:	Experimental Record:
		Obstacles Parking Lot

Figure 17.1   Starting the Kata Storyboard.

"It may be," Linda acknowledged. "Remember, you're also learning how to improve at the same time you're working on the improvements. It's like learning any new skill. Most people can't learn a new skill all at once. Usually you must take small steps, practice them, get coaching on what you're doing well and what needs to change, and eventually, you will master the skill." She looked around the group. "Who will be working on this challenge?"

"I will," said Mo. "And I think we need one other contact center person, and because we will be reducing the use of the app, IT. So, Erica, you're our IT partner, I guess that is you." A young woman from the contact center, Elizabeth, raised her hand shyly. "Thanks, Elizabeth!" Beth smiled to herself. She had been concerned about Elizabeth's participation. She was quiet, and had great success handling unhappy customers, but in the team, she was often passive, seemed unengaged in the contact center social life, and rarely spoke up in meetings.

Linda wrote the names in her notebook and on the whiteboard.

"Linda, I have a question," said Mo. "To remember our creative thinking perspective, can we restate that challenge as a question?"

"If you like," Linda replied. "How do you want to say it?"

"How might we reduce inbound complaint call volume to less than 500/day?" Mo picked up a whiteboard marker. "I'll change it on the board if everyone agrees." Seeing the heads nodding, he rewrote the challenge.

Focus Process: *Incoming Call Handling*		Challenge: *How might we reduce Inbound Complaint Call Volume less than 500/day? Mo, Elizabeth and Erica*
Target Condition: *840 complaint calls a day* Achieve By: *October 15*	Current Condition:: *980 complaint calls a day*	Experimental Record:
		Obstacles Parking Lot

Figure 17.2 Continuing the Kata Storyboard.

Linda turned back to the storyboard. "Let's do the call volume target condition. What is your target condition for call volume? And when do you want to achieve it? Remember when we played with the puzzles? We didn't try to achieve the goal, the challenge, right away."

Mo and the group conferred for a moment. "We're going to aim for reducing call volume by 10 percent within one month."

"What call volume would that be?"

Mo scribbled on a piece of paper. "840 complaint calls a day. Down from our 980-complaint call average."

Linda nodded and handed the marker to Elizabeth. "Add that to your storyboard. And the three of you can add your current data."

Elizabeth added the data from the A3. The whole group stood back and looked at the board. "What obstacles are preventing you from achieving your target condition?" Linda asked. "I know if Carlo were here, he would advise you to think divergently to generate that list."

"Ah, I see," said Mo. "We can use divergent thinking to come up with the list of obstacles and convergent thinking to select the first one to work on."

"Right," said Linda. "You're going to use your data to spur the divergent thinking and use the target condition and the goal as the guidance for 'being deliberate' when you perform your convergent thinking. And you can take a similar divergent and convergent thinking approach when you determine what experiment you will try first. When will the three of you be able to work on the obstacles and the next experiment?"

"We'll do it this afternoon," said Mo enthusiastically. "You can take a look tomorrow morning."

Linda nodded. "Perfect. Let's work on the rest of these objectives. Mo, you said, that you expected that contact center associates would be helping customers with their orders. Tell me more about that."

"We know that many of our customers are not going to use the app, or their computer to order parts. So, we would like to offer a new call-in line for those customers. But we don't really know what it will take to do that effectively."

"That is like you're creating a new product, in a way," said Linda. "Although you can use the kata for new product development, we should take a different approach initially. And Carlo could help us as well." She looked at the other aspirations that Mo had stated. "You know, two of these other ones are also more like new products: 'proactively reaching out to customers' and 'providing better analytics.'"

"Does that mean we can't take a lean approach to them?" Mo looked worried.

"Yes, you can take a lean approach. It is a little different, but everything you have learned so far, PDCA, A3s, the improvement kata, and CPS will help."

Beth smiled to herself again. Mo seemed to be stepping up well to lead this work. She wanted to see him delegate some of the other objectives to others to lead, but there was time to make sure he wasn't behaving like Beth and trying to drive everything himself.

"When we get to employee satisfaction," said Jeremy, "I want to be part of that."

"Sounds good, Jeremy," said Mo. "Let's work on that one next, Linda."

"Mo sounds like a leader to me," thought Beth. She was happy to see that she didn't need to be part of the conversation for people to make progress.

PRACTICE THIS TODAY

Is it clear to you which segment of your work is "improvement projects" and which are really about creating a "new product?" What might you do to improve your approach to the new product work in your organization?

Chapter 18

A New Product

Beth caught up with Linda outside the meeting room. The rest of the meeting had gone well, and the contact center now had two teams working on challenges related to creating a Center for Customer Experience. While Beth was happy with the progress, and Mo's leadership, and Jeremy's participation, she was concerned about the three challenges for which Linda had not created storyboards.

"Linda, I need more insight about why those three challenges got left off the table today. I was hoping we could get multiple teams kicked off."

"Do you agree that those challenges are more like the creation of new products than improvements of existing processes?"

"I guess so. But it's not like we're setting out to design a new flange or faucet."

"True, it's not a physical product. But the contact center is about to create something for internal and external customers that essentially doesn't exist. There is nothing in place to improve." Linda sighed. "I believe that there are new product aspects to the reduction of call volume as well. There will need to be a new process to let other departments know about processes that they need to improve. But some of that will be taken care of by the development of the new analytical function and the new reports, which is one of our 'new product' projects. You and Mo will need to make sure that the teams working on these challenges stay in communication."

Beth's stomach growled and she looked at her phone. It was lunchtime. "Are you free for a quick bite, Linda? Can you fill me in on lean product development?"

They made their way to the cafeteria, bought some lunch, and found Carlo returning to his "office' from another meeting. He waved to them and they sat down together. "How did it go this morning? I missed you guys, but there is so much going on around here – I can't be everywhere."

"It was good," said Beth. "But we didn't get all the challenges quantified and on a storyboard. Linda observed that some of the challenges were more like new products than improvement projects. I asked her to give me a quick explanation of lean product development, so I know what is going to happen next. I guess I'm also wondering how CPS would play into that. Although I'd guess that divergent thinking is a key part of coming up with new product ideas."

Carlo nodded vigorously; "Yes, of course, and convergent thinking as well. But it all starts with understanding and clarifying what problem you're solving for the customer."

"I think this is where CPS and lean have tremendous synergy," said Linda. "Lean product development is focused on developing people who can create products that bring value to their customers. And, of course, to do that, you need to understand the customer well, and know what problem you're solving for them. In my opinion, when you look at approaches like lean product development, lean start-up, design thinking, and Creative Problem Solving, there is a tremendous amount of overlap."

"I'm not sure I agree with that," said Carlo, "but I don't think our methodological arguments are helpful to Beth."

"I have no idea what you're talking about anyway," said Beth.

"What do you know about product development?" asked Linda.

"Not much. It's not really a function we have at GPS."

"Have you observed what happens when companies come out with new products? Are they all successful?"

Beth thought about recent news stories she had seen. A new soda flavor, announced with a lot of hype, disappearing from the market in a couple of months. A blockbuster movie that had lost millions. A new aircraft plagued by technical problems.

"No, I guess they are not. Some even cause their companies to lose money."

Linda pulled her notebook from her bag and pushed her lunch tray aside. "Think about this idea of a dedicated call-in line for customers to order products over the phone. Sounds like a great idea, right? Everyone here at GPS loves it. But to Carlo's point, we don't know yet if it solves a customer need."

Beth was taken aback. "But we know some of our customers are not going to use the app, even if we fix it."

"Hmmm … have you asked any customers? Do you know what problem they need to have solved?"

"I know I have heard some customers say that they don't use smartphones and that they can't access computers when they are at a worksite, so it seems logical that a call-in line would be great for them. But I get what you're saying, because I have done this so many times myself, confusing a favorite solution with understanding the real problem. Shouldn't we tell Mo and the team?"

Linda shook her head. "We can trust the process to do that for them, and they will learn better because of it, and they will learn pretty soon."

"Then what is the process?"

Linda drew a picture in her notebook. "This is a typical product development process. In this process, decisions about the products, its features and how to deliver it are 'locked in' early, and if any of those decisions are wrong, the product will be late, and may not be successful."

She drew a large arrow above the process. "Developing a new product involves a lot of learning, and in the typical process, the learning happens late in the process and can be very expensive. You can think of it as doing all the learning in a large batch."

Beth leaned forward to look at the drawing. "And, in lean, we try to avoid large batches."

"You got it," Linda said. "So, in a lean product development process, we try to keep our learning in small batches, by performing short learning cycles. These are basically PDCA cycles. Another principle has to do with

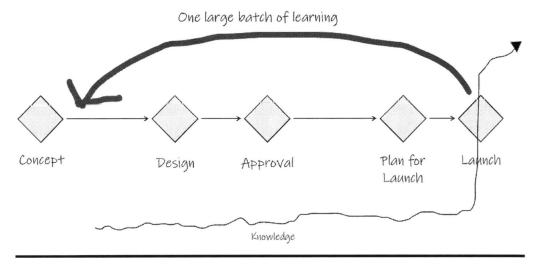

Figure 18.1   One Large Batch of Learning.

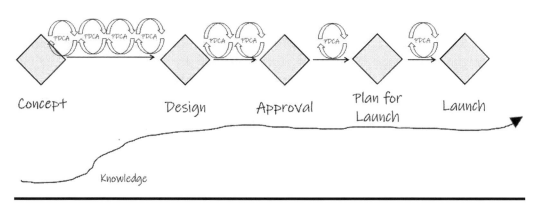

Figure 18.2   Many Small Batches of Learning.

waste. In this case, we're talking about waste of knowledge gained during the learning. There is no value to customers or to product developers if we must keep learning the same lesson. In lean product development, we capture as much learning as we can in each learning cycle, often in A3s. This helps to speed up the development and delivery of subsequent products."

She drew another picture in her notebook. "A lean product development process will look like this."

Beth tapped the picture. "How do we know what we need to learn, and when?"

"Great question, Beth!" Linda looked at Carlo. "Many lean product development practitioners do a divergent thinking exercise at the beginning of the process, listing all the questions they have about the customer, the product, its features, technical issues, etc. They then use a convergent thinking approach such as an evaluation matrix or a risk assessment to determine which questions are most important to answer early, and to decide whether any can be answered concurrently or with information they already have. This allows them to plan the key decisions they need to make, and that drives which learning cycles to perform, and when. Of course, as they learn, they may generate additional questions, and that might change the plan. In a typical product development plan, the focus is on execution, and new learnings are not accounted for."

"Interesting," said Beth, "and because the learning cycles are PDCA cycles, there will be times when CPS tools can help with the thinking. And you could use the improvement kata as well. But it seems all this upfront work would make the process longer."

Linda shook her head. "Haven't we had this conversation before?"

Beth knew what Linda was talking about. "I guess if we deliver entirely the wrong product, it doesn't matter how long the process takes, all our work is wasted. Which kind of reminds me of the ordering app. We spent so much time and money on that and it's almost all been wasted."

Linda nodded her head in agreement. "Right. And once you're locked into major decisions – say, implementing a new app or hiring and training people to take customer orders over the phone, and you find that it is not going deliver the value you expected, it will take you longer to get to the right answer and it will be considerably more expensive."

"We would have to figure out what to do with those people we hired."

Carlo leaned over to look at the drawings. "I have to say, this is fascinating. I can imagine a lot of ways to use CPS tools in this process. A natural fit. It needs to start with customer knowledge, right, Linda? What are the ways the team can get that customer knowledge?"

Linda and Beth both laughed. "Where are your sticky notes, Carlo?" Beth exclaimed. "We need to brainstorm!"

"Let's get a few more people together to do that. I will check with Mo to find out who he wants and when."

Linda tapped the picture she had drawn of the lean product development process. "Beth, I have given you a very high-level explanation. There is a lot more to this. If you're interested, I can recommend …"

"Another book, right? I'll take it. Even though I'm not a product developer."

"Ah, but you are," said Carlo. "You and Mo and the contact center are bringing something entirely new to the company. You're a product developer."

PRACTICE THIS TODAY

How does the creation of new offerings or products work in your organization? How early do you make decisions and what is the result of making those decisions early? Where are you using divergent thinking? Where are you using convergent thinking?

Chapter 19

Not A Typical Monday

"Did you hear?" asked Georgia, in a low tone, as she pushed the button on the coffee machine. "We have an all hands meeting this afternoon."

Beth had her head in the refrigerator, looking for half-and-half. "Why don't we have a kanban for the coffee supplies?" she thought to herself.

"Yes, I know, Georgia. It is not a big deal. Well, Brandon does have an announcement to make, but it is a good one."

Georgia stirred her coffee so vigorously it spilled on the counter. "Can you tell me?"

"No way!" Beth laughed. "If I tell you, it will be all over the company by lunch time, and then Brandon won't need the meeting, and all the refreshments he ordered will need to be sent back."

Beth couldn't find any half and half, so she settled for a cup of cold water. She walked briskly through the building and entered the warehouse. The warehouse team was already circled around their visual board. She had almost missed the daily meeting.

"Hi, Beth!" exclaimed Keisha. "You're just in time. Judy is going to lead the meeting today."

"Judy looks great," Beth thought. Judy had been back at work for three months now and had recently given up the cane she had been using since her return.

Judy spoke to the assembled group. "Good morning, everyone, and happy Monday! First, let's do the numbers from Saturday. We had 2,165 orders on Saturday, and they were all picked and shipped by noon. We had no safety incidents and received no complaints about wrong shipments. It was a good day!" There was a smattering of applause. Judy continued. "Today we have 4,003 orders to pick and expect to receive another 400 or so rush orders from the contact center. We're fully staffed today …" there was another wave of applause, "and today we welcome our high school summer intern, Connor Brickell." Beth smiled at Connor, who ignored her pointedly. "Are there any issues to report?" Judy looked around the group.

Keisha pointed at a card held on the board by a red magnet. "Who owns this one?"

A young woman that Beth didn't know raised her hand. "We're running low on the SKUs from Neptune Industries. Their shipment was due Thursday and it hasn't arrived. A couple of those SKUs are in the supermarket and are below the kanban for replenishment."

Judy asked, "What do we know about this problem?"

The young woman continued. "I contacted Neptune and they said that their invoices are not getting paid on time, so they are withholding shipments until they are paid."

Keisha picked up the card. "I will take this to the managers' meeting, and make sure that Accounts Payable is up to speed."

Judy looked around the group. "Who can work with Letitia on options for managing this situation until we can get a shipment?" Several people raised their hands. "Letitia, how soon can we hear what the viable options are?"

"We will have an answer this afternoon. 2 p.m."

"And I will report back on what Accounts Payable says this afternoon as well," said Keisha. "Don't forget we have an all hands meeting at 3 p.m."

Beth thought back to how this would have been handled a year ago. Most likely, no one would have known about the shortage until a customer had requested some of those SKUs and they wouldn't have been able to fill the order. If they had learned that there was an apparent issue with invoices not being paid, there might have been angry emails or phone calls to Accounts Payable. Beth would have been drawn into the emails and phone calls, and perhaps difficult meetings where blame was passed around the room like a hot potato. Now they were able to see the problem, communicate it effectively to Accounts Payable, and help each other with creative solutions. She expected that Accounts Payable would take the information from Keisha with equanimity and quickly work to solve the problem, and Beth wouldn't need to be involved at all.

She took another look at Connor. She realized he wouldn't appreciate being told how adorable he looked in his hard hat and safety glasses. That was another thing. A year ago, she would not have wanted her son working in this warehouse. Now she was confident in his safety, and that he would learn valuable lean thinking and creative thinking tools that would only benefit his future education and career.

She stepped outside and walked briskly across the parking lot to the Customer Experience Center. The first shift was just finishing their morning meeting when she arrived. She hung back until the meeting was finished. "Mo, can you give me a quick review of today's meeting?" she asked.

Mo reviewed their visual board with her. Like the warehouse, they had no absences, and most of the metrics were within the expected range. Mo showed her one graph he was especially happy with: call handling time.

"As you can see, Beth, incoming call volume is continuing to decline. Now that we know what the most common customer issue are and have eliminated them, we're close to our goal. But look at call handling time!"

The line on the graph was getting steadily higher. "As you can see, the call handling time is continuing to increase. We're finding that customers want to spend more time on the phone with their Customer Experience Representative, and we think that is translating into more sales and more positive referrals."

"Do you know that relationship for sure?" Beth asked.

"We're still exploring that. The sales folks think so, and sales are going up, but I can't say for sure yet." Mo took her around to see several kata story boards. In the early spring, the Customer Experience Center had invited sales, marketing, the warehouse, IT, and HR to a workshop on integrating process across the functions. Several projects were underway, and almost everyone was involved in a project, either as a participant or as a coach. Beth could tell that one of the groups had been brainstorming together because one wall was covered in colorful sticky notes.

"Are you excited for this afternoon?" Beth asked. Mo was one of the few people outside the directors who knew what was going to be announced at the all hands meeting.

"I am! And nervous. How do you like being a director?"

"It is a big change. I still have a lot to learn. New types of problems to solve. I miss Roberta every day, but I talked to her last week, and she is very happy out there on the West Coast."

Beth checked the time on her phone. It was almost time for the managers' morning meeting. "Want to walk over with me, Mo?"

Outside, it was beginning to get hot, and the air was humid. They were glad to get back into the air conditioning. Beth checked her fitness tracker; she had already walked a mile and half. That was another difference from a year ago. Now she was no longer shackled to her computer, answering emails and juggling meetings. After the managers' meeting, she would head to the directors' meeting. By 9:30 a.m., she would know almost everything going on in the company. She planned to go back to the Center for Customer Experience and sit in on a brainstorming session and later she had a coaching meeting planned with Mo.

At 3:00 p.m., the cafeteria was packed. Brandon stood on a small platform, looking relaxed and happy. Beth found a spot near the platform.

"Hello, GPS!" Brandon greeted his employees.

"Hello, Brandon!"

"I'm very happy that so many of you could be here this afternoon and a big hello to our new West Coast team who are joining us on video." A screen behind Brandon showed the small group of West Coast employees waving to the camera.

"About a year ago, we started on a journey to improve our company. The directors and I had an off-site meeting, and we set some ambitious goals for the company. And I need to tell you that we had no idea how we were going to reach them. But I knew how smart you all are, and I knew we could all learn to learn better together, to be more creative together, and most importantly, come together to serve our customers.

"I'd like to tell you today that we have achieved all those goals. But we haven't – yet. Those goals are three-year goals and we've only been on this journey for one year. Our progress has been outstanding this far, even though we have faced some enormous challenges, and we will have more in the future. I'm so proud of all of you for everything you have done, and the changes you have embraced. I'm looking forward to what happens next."

Brandon motioned to someone to join him on the stage. Beth smiled as she watched Mo emerge from the crowd and step up to the platform. "One year ago," Brandon said, "we were considering some pretty drastic moves. We knew there was at least one department that needed, let's say, a lot of change. But this guy," – he indicated Mo, "and his team took on that change, and they changed all of us. They took a bold step, decided to get out in front and lead, with a heart for the customer and the courage to be creative. So, Mohammed Khan, I would like to present you, and the Center for Customer Experience, with the first annual GPS change-maker award." Mo looked thoroughly thrilled, and completely embarrassed by the applause and cheering. Brandon handed him a large trophy shaped like a J-bend pipe.

"In honor of this team's accomplishments, we're celebrating with ice cream sundaes. I think you folks in San Jose have ice cream too?"

Beth slipped out of the room, and found Carlo and Linda chatting in the hallway. Carlo waved her over. "Our favorite student!"

"Did you see the presentation?" Beth asked.

"We did," said Linda. "You must be very proud of Mo."

"It wasn't me; it was you two that made it happen."

Linda shook her head. "No, it was Mo and you. We gave him a way to think, and tools to work with. You supported and coached him well. You listened to him, gave him space, and safety, and got out of your own way and his way so that he could innovate."

"Well, thank you, I guess," Beth responded. "I feel as if I have learned more than anyone."

"Beth, you know, our contracts are almost over. We will always be available to you, but going forward, GPS will be standing on its own feet. Will you keep learning?"

"Can I get you back to facilitate if I need you?"

Linda reached out and patted Beth's shoulder. "Probably. But our job has been to *build* your capability, not *be* your capability."

"What am I going to do without you?"

Carlo cleared his throat. Beth knew what that meant. "No, what I mean is, 'how might I continue to build my skills?'"

"Good question, Beth. Need some sticky notes?"

"That's okay," said Beth. "I already have some ideas."

Afterword

Beth's story is a fable. It is not a recipe for a lean transformation. Few would attempt to teach and implement all these lean approaches and CPS across an organization in less than a year! It is also a fable because lean transformation is hard.

GPS has the benefit of engaged leadership and people at all levels willing to make a change in the way they work and think and even care about each other. Wherever you are in your lean journey, be prepared to test every assumption you have about how organizations work and how people should behave. And be prepared to use creative thinking to move your lean transformation forward.

Appendix 1

A Brief History of Creative Problem Solving

You have undoubtedly been in a meeting and somebody has said, "Let's brainstorm on this." Or somebody has started to list some ideas and said (often as an apology), "I'm just brainstorming." Or perhaps you've heard, "Brainstorming doesn't work!" Where did that term come from?

Before 1939, a "brain storm" meant a sudden fit of melancholy, or an epileptic seizure! But in 1939, something happened to change the definition to a more positive meaning. An American advertising executive, Alex Faickney Osborn, started to get groups of his colleagues at the agency BBDO (Batten, Barten, Durstine, & Osborn) together to generate creative ideas for advertising campaigns.[1] The groups followed specific rules for these sessions, which they started to call "brainstorm sessions." The results of these sessions provided their clients with innovative advertising that made BBDO a leading agency in the US.

Osborn realized that there was more to learn (and teach) about creativity, and in the 1950s, he partnered with Sid Parnes, a professor of psychology at Buffalo State College to develop and document the "Osborn-Parnes Creative Solving Problem Process." It was this process that evolved into "CPS." Osborn and Parnes founded the Creative Education Foundation (CEF), a non-profit organization, whose mission is to "spark personal and professional transformation by empowering people with the skill set, tool set, and mindset of deliberate creativity" (www.creativeeducationfoundation. org/about-cef/). They also founded the International Center for Studies in Creativity at Buffalo State College (now SUNY Buffalo State), which offers a master's program in Creativity Studies.

Amazingly, Osborn and Parnes and their successors saw this as a gift to the world and did not copyright or patent the CPS process. At the Center for Creative Studies and at CEF, research continues into human creativity and its use to solve problems of every size. Every summer, hundreds of learners meet in Buffalo, NY, to advance their knowledge of CPS and share their learning from implementation across a wide range of industries, educational institutions, and even governmental organizations. Elements from CPS have found their way into many other methodologies.

Brainstorming was a key ideation technique in the new CPS process, but brainstorming was only one piece of the creative thinking puzzle. Osborn and Parnes thought through and experimented with how and when to use brainstorming and related approaches to generate and develop ideas, and how to evaluate, select from, and strengthen the many ideas generated.

They determined that it was critically important to separate and balance the work of coming up with ideas (divergent thinking) from the work of selecting ideas to move forward, which they referred to as "judgment" (convergent thinking).

> Separate Divergent Thinking
> from
> Convergent Thinking

They also realized that they could waste a lot of time and effort if they tried to solve a poorly understood problem.

Alex Osborn initially proposed a problem-solving process with seven stages which were later condensed to three stages (fact-finding, idea-finding, and solution-finding). Note that there is no stage to "plan for implementation."

In early versions of CPS, the focus was on divergent thinking, so much so that in 1953, Alex Osborn added a chapter to a revision of his work "Applied Imagination," stressing the importance of "judicial thinking," although most of the chapter is apologetics for the necessity of focusing on divergent thinking in earlier versions of the book.[2]

CPS's evolution led to creative thinkers using both divergent thinking and convergent thinking in a more balanced way, tapping into both their ability to ideate and their skills of judgment. As CPS has evolved over the years, different versions and models of the process have been created, with varying numbers of steps displayed using linear models, spirals, and many other creative graphical approaches. (To read about one modern version of CPS, see Appendix 4.) As new models for CPS were developed, practitioners also developed dozens of tools to assist in divergent and convergent thinking. These tools are powerful when used inside the creative problem-solving process, and they are just as powerful when used with any of the lean problem-solving approaches. Learn more about some of these tools in Appendices 2 and 3.

Osborn and Parnes did not stop with tools. Over the course of their collaboration, they investigated many factors potentially impacting creativity: age (older people make more interesting connections between ideas, perhaps due to longer experience), gender (they found women to be better than men at brainstorming), education, emotions, exposure to the arts, habits, the need for the subconscious to incubate ideas; all this before neuroscience began to delve into creativity. One key creative thinking concept woven through their work regards questions.

Every discovery starts with a question. "What is over that hill? Why does the sun appear to travel across the sky? How might we prevent people from falling ill?" The practice of *affirmative inquiry* is woven through CPS. Challenges, problems, issues are stated as questions inviting a positive and creative response. CPS practitioners use sentence starters (stems) like "How might …?" or "What are the ways …?" together with a positive outcome statement to state challenges and issues. There is a big difference between saying "I am always late to work," and "How might I get to work on time?"

Affirmative inquiry elicits a creative response.

In preparing to write this, I acquired a copy of Alex Osborn's *Applied Imagination: Principles and Procedures of Creative Thinking* (the 1953 revision). The copy I got from a used bookseller is slightly musty and the pages are yellowed. In one sense, it is dated: most of the time, he refers to "men" rather than to people. But how modern this book seems otherwise! Like the latest edition of the *Harvard Business Review*, Osborn tells of companies that have benefitted from creating climates that permit risk-taking and which value the creative ability of every employee at every level.

Why so little is known by lean practitioners of the work of Osborn and Parnes is a mystery; is it because once we learn about lean, we focus exclusively on learning more about lean?

Notes

1. Osborn, Alex F., *Your Creative Power: How to Use Imagination* (New York: Charles Scribner's Sons, 1948).
2. Osborn, Alex F., *Applied Imagination: Principles and Procedures of Creative Thinking* (New York: Charles Scribner's Sons, 1957).

Appendix 2

Rules and Tools for Divergent Thinking

All tools for divergent thinking are based on brainstorming. Divergent thinking tools can obviously be used to generate ideas when we need a solution or countermeasure, or a product idea, and we need to think divergently in many situations and steps of the Creative Problem Solving process. Tools for divergent thinking can also be used to generate everything from vision statements to data, to ideas, to lists of assisters and resisters when planning implementation. In this Appendix you will find descriptions of brainstorming and three other tools. You can find more tools for divergent thinking in the *Creative Problem Solving Tools & Techniques Resource Guide* (www.creativeeducationfoundation.org/wp-content/uploads/2015/06/ToolsTechniques-Guide-FINAL-web-watermark.pdf), which you can download free from the Creative Education Foundation website. CEF has more free tools at www.creativeeducationfoundation.org/resources/facilitation-tools/

Brainstorming and the other tools for divergent thinking are often used as described in this book in a group or team setting. You can of course brainstorm on your own too!

The Rules (Guidelines) for Divergent Thinking are critical to success. If you are facilitating a divergent thinking session, teach the rules before you start, and refer to them frequently. As a facilitator, the rules apply to you too. Even saying "good one!" when you hear an idea can dampen people's creative output, as they may then want to compete in pleasing you.

If you can, post the guidelines in the room.

GUIDELINES FOR DIVERGENT THINKING

Defer Judgment
Combine and Build
Seek Wild Ideas
Go for Quantity

Brainstorming

A brainstorming session requires at a minimum one human being and a topic that needs ideas or options, but brainstorming is usually performed in a group setting.

You probably noticed that Carlo used sticky notes. These are easy to display, and easy to sort and rearrange when it is time to practice convergent thinking. Using sticky notes also has the advantage of allowing more introverted or shyer members of your group a little cover for their initial ideas. If you need to brainstorm and you don't have a pad of sticky notes, scraps of paper or index cards will do just fine.

Begin the session by stating the goal for the session and reviewing the rules for divergent thinking. You can give the group a warm-up exercise, such as coming with ideas for using a shoebox, or improving a bedroom. During the warm-up, encourage the group to keep coming up with ideas. (You might want to give them a goal, like 100 ideas, which helps them to strive for quantity.) Read ideas out loud as they are generated, and ask questions like "What does that make you think of?" Periodically ask "What else?"

If you are posting the sticky notes on a flipchart sheet or wall, keep them organized in neat rows and columns. This will help you count the sticky notes and make them easy to read when it is time for convergent thinking. Read as many of the ideas out loud as possible as you collect them and place them on the wall or flipchart sheet. For your convenience, number flipchart sheets and make sure the topic of the brainstorm is written on each sheet. Once you have generated several flipchart sheets on several topics, you will be very glad you did this!

Once the group is warmed-up, make sure the topic of the brainstorming session is clearly displayed, and announce it. Make sure that you use the correct statement starter depending on the step you are in. (For example, when stating challenges/issues, make sure they are using a "stem" that will allow them to state the challenge as a question.)

How do you know when to stop? Pushing beyond initial ideas is often necessary to get novel ideas or combinations of ideas. So, don't stop when you first feel the group energy slowing down. You can go back and read out previous ideas/options out loud to spur twists on those ideas. Ask the group to think how ideas might be combined. Or use one or more of the tools below to keep ideas/options flowing.

Brainwriting

Brainwriting is a modified version of brainstorming developed by Horst Geschka. Unlike brainstorming with stickies, which involves saying ideas or options out loud as they are generated, brainwriting is done silently. Prepare by applying sticky notes to sheets of paper in rows (three rows and three columns). Participants write ideas/options on the stickies, and after they have completed a row, they exchange sheets or pass them around. Seeing other people's thinking on the sheet and building on their options then spurs another round of divergent thinking.

Forced Connections

Forced connections is a tool used in a brainstorming session to help participants see the topic from a different perspective, which then invites novel ideas/options.

Show participants an object or a picture and ask them to consider and if needed, state out loud, the attributes of the object or picture. Then ask them to force a mental connection between those attributes and topic they are working on. (Carlo used forced connections in Chapter 17.) Forced connections is a tool that is handy for spurring more ideas/options when a group seems to be lagging in energy, and when a group seems to be stuck on conventional ideas. Be ready with some pictures, objects, or concepts to share. Brainstorming by yourself? You can still use forced connections. Look at the pictures on your wall, or an object in your office or home. Even a stapler or a tennis ball will do.

SCAMPER

Scamper was developed by Robert (Bob) Eberle from a set of questions originally used by Alex Osborn (Eberle, 1971). Scamper stands for:

Substitute
Combine
Adapt
Modify
Put to other uses
Eliminate
Rearrange

Ask questions based on these themes to help a group generate variations on their ideas/options, or if a group seems to be stuck. For example, ask, what could we substitute for a component or feature? How might we combine options? Is there something we could adapt from another field of expertise? How might some options be modified (or made bigger, or smaller or more flexible)? Which ideas might be put to other uses? Is there a feature/process that could be eliminated? What would happen if we rearranged some components/steps? Prepare by generating your own list of questions.

SCAMPER

Substitute
Combine
Adapt
Modify
Put to other uses
Eliminate
Rearrange

References

Eberle, R. F. (1971) *Games for Imagination Development*. Buffalo, NY: DOK.

Osborn, A. F. (1963) Brainstorming and Forced Connection. In *Applied Imagination: Principles and Procedures of Creative Problem-Solving* (3rd ed.). New York: Scribner.

Vehar, J., Miller, B., and Firestien, R. (2001) *Creativity Unbound: An Introduction to Creative Problem-Solving*. Evanston, IL: THinc Communications.

Appendix 3

Rules and Tools for Convergent Thinking

Creative problem-solving practitioners have created many tools for convergent thinking. Convergent thinking includes:

- Evaluating ideas or options.
- Selecting ideas or options.
- Strengthening ideas or options.
- Prioritizing options.

Each of these operations demands a different type of tool. Five tools are described here. You can find more tools for convergent thinking in the *Creative Problem Solving Tools & Techniques Resource Guide* (www.creativeeducationfoundation.org/wp-content/uploads/2015/06/ToolsTechniques-Guide-FINAL-web-watermark.pdf), which you can download free from the Creative Education Foundation website. CEF has more free tools at www.creativeeducationfoundation.org/resources/facilitation-tools/

The guidelines for convergent thinking should be reviewed before using any tool.

GUIDELINES FOR CONVERGENT THINKING

Be Deliberate
Check Your Objectives
Improve Your Ideas
Be Affirmative
Consider Novelty

Highlighting

Highlighting is a tool for selecting and in some cases prioritizing ideas or options. It is very useful when there are many options to work through. The first part of highlighting is selecting Hits in order to reduce the number of options. Many people use dots for selecting hits, but you can use anything that allows you distinguish the highlighted ideas or options, such as marking a colored mark on a sticky note. It is a good idea to review all the options before highlighting starts. Participants are asked to mark the option that they like best or are most novel or somehow sparkles for them. Sometimes you will want to generate and select criteria to help select options. (Make sure that everyone has the same number of dots.)

Clustering

Clustering is the next step in highlighting but can also be done independently of highlighting. In clustering, ideas or options that are related are grouped together. It is very important to do this carefully. It is easy for participants to try to cluster based on similar words. Help them to discern items with related meanings, not just similar words, by asking what an item is about or what it means to the person who wrote it. Once a group of ideas or options has been clustered, restate the cluster with the appropriate type of phrase to the stage you are working in (for example, if you are working on issues, restate the cluster as a question). The goal is to only cluster those options that are closely related. Some options will stand alone.

POINt

POINt is a variation of the PPCO technique that was developed by Diane Foucar-Szocki, Bill Shepard, and Roger Firestien in 1982 (Vehar, Miller, and Fierstien, 2001). POINt is a tool for evaluating and strengthening ideas or options. Because it starts with praise, it is useful whenever an idea, option or proposal may face resistance before a fair evaluation. It is best used when only a small number of options are in consideration – two or three at most.

POINt stands for:

Pluses
Opportunities
Issues
New **T**hinking.

Start by asking participants to state what they like about the idea or option

Then what it could lead to (Opportunities). Opportunities can be stated with the stem "It might."

Issue are stated as affirmative questions, "How might?" or "In what ways might?"

New thinking is generating ideas for solutions to the issues (a divergent thinking activity in a convergent thinking tool!).

Finally, the original idea or option is restated to include the result of the "new thinking" activity. POINt can be a lengthy activity but it can also be run through quickly when an idea or option needs some support to get it past initial skepticism.

The Evaluation Matrix

The evaluation matrix is a useful tool for selection and evaluation and even strengthening of options (Noller, Parnes, and Biondi, 1976). You can use it to compare several ideas and to evaluate them against pre-selected criteria. Start by selecting criteria important to the problem or project (you might need to go through a cycle of divergent and convergent thinking to determine the criteria). Ideally, state each criterion as a question requiring a positive answer for success. For example, "Can it be completed in six months?" or "Will it be possible to build using existing technology?"

You also need to decide how to rate each option against the criteria (you could color-code them, for example). Once the matrix is filled in, you can compare your options. You may see some that could be easily strengthened (back to divergent thinking!) and you can also see when options might be combined to create a set of complementary countermeasures.

A Risk/Impact matrix is a version of an evaluation matrix that is helpful for prioritization in product development, once a list of development questions has been generated. Each question is evaluated according to whether a negative answer to the question is perceived as having a low, medium, or high risk of occurring, and whether the impact of a negative answer would have a low, medium, or high impact to the success of the project. Questions with a high-risk score and a high impact score should be answered as soon as technically feasible.

Targeting

Targeting was developed by Blair Miller and Gerard Puccio of the International Center for Studies in Creativity. Targeting is a tool that can be

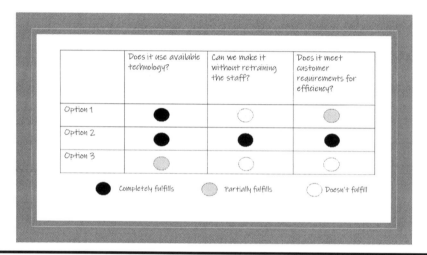

Figure A3.1   Evaluation Matrix.

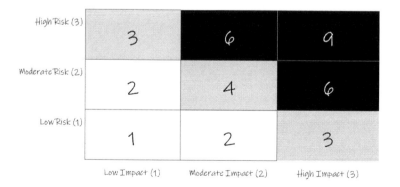

Figure A3.2   Risk/Impact Matrix.

used to evaluate how well options meet pre-selected criteria or, as shown in this book, to help drive support and buy-in for a planned solution or countermeasure. Draw a target on a wall and determine or state what the center of the target means (full support for the proposal or complete satisfaction of project criteria, for example).

In the case of ideas, discuss where each idea should be placed on the target. Ask, "What would it take to move it to the center of the target?" Similarly, when using the target to develop support for a proposal, ask, "What would it take to move your support for this proposal to the center of the target?" Note that what brings one participant closer to full support may cause another participant to withdraw their support. You might need to affirmatively restate a question such as "How might we meet both people's needs?" after which you will need to further strengthen the proposal to get full agreement.

References

Firestein, R. L. and Trefinger, D. J. (1983) Highlighting. *Journal of Creative Behavior, Ownership and Converging: Ingredients of Creative Problem Solving*, 17(1): 32–38.

Miller, B. and Puccio, G. (2001) *Creativity Unbound: An Introduction to Creative Problem-Solving*. Evanston, IL: THinc Communications.

Noller, R. B., Parnes, S. J., and Biondi, A. M. (1976) *Creative Action Book*. New York: Scribner's Sons.

Vehar, J., Miller, B., and Firestien, R. (2001) *Creativity Unbound: An Introduction to Creative Problem-Solving*. Evanston, IL: THinc Communications.

Appendix 4

Creative Problem Solving in Practice

Creative Problem Solving (CPS) is used widely across industry, government, non-profit organizations, academia, and in education. Because it is so widely used, there are many published versions of the CPS process. If you are a lean thinker, using a lean problem-solving approach, understanding how CPS is used in practice may enrich your understanding of your lean problem-solving approach.

The Creative Education Foundation proposes a 'learner's model" with four stages (clarify, ideate, develop, implement) and six steps, starting with identifying a goal, wish or challenge and ending with exploring acceptance and identifying assisters and resisters of implementing the selected solutions. In each of the six steps, there is a phase of divergent thinking and convergent thinking. Like a PDCA cycle, this is visually depicted as a cycle.[1]

A CPS model like this can be used to help an organization find and plan to implement a strategic direction, or to create and plan to implement solutions for new products. In a lean organization, PDCA cycles might then be used to implement the strategy or to develop the new product. But this process doesn't need to be used as part of a formal initiative or project.

Where there is a need to solve a problem, and you own it, and it requires some imagination, you can apply CPS. The following is an example of an individual application of CPS. Imagine you are faced with a decision about your career.

You could start by **identifying your goal, wish or challenge**. Brainstorm using the stem, "It would be great if …"

Now do some convergent thinking to select the goal that you want to work on at this time. Which ones are the most exciting to you? Which would be best for your family? Once you are clear on your goal/wish/challenge, it is time to **gather data** about the situation. For example, what kind of jobs are there that would satisfy your goal? Where are they? Who has a job like this? What education, training, and experience do they require? Use convergent thinking to sort through the data. Use the data to **formulate key challenges** (problems) you need to solve in order to achieve your goal. State the challenges as questions which implies that they can be overcome with new thinking (for example, "How might I find connections in Tahiti?").

For each challenge, **generate ideas** to answer the question. Use convergent thinking tools to **select the best ideas, develop them into solutions, then evaluate and develop the solutions**.

Finally, you will need to **plan to implement** your solution. Think divergently. Who can help you? What will help you? Who might resist? Think divergently again: how might you overcome that resistance? Now you are ready to generate all the actions you need to take. Use convergent thinking to select and prioritize your actions. Now you are ready to complete your plan for implementation.

Much like the use of CPS tools can enhance your lean thinking approaches, lean thinking can be used to enhance CPS. As a lean thinker, you will find points in this process to run PDCA cycles. You might want to verify your data, run some iterations on a solution that looks promising, or experiment with various approaches to overcome resistance. If your career exploration leads you to develop new skills, you could use the improvement kata to support and track your progress in developing those skills.

Like lean thinking, there are several models and frameworks for Creative Problem Solving. One that some lean thinkers will find interesting is the "thinking skills" model proposed by Gerard Puccio and his colleagues Marie Mance and Mary C. Murdock. This model places "gathering data" and "assessing the situation" in the center of a three-stage process presented as a circle.[2] The three stages (clarification, transformation, and implementation) include six steps. Puccio, Mance, and Murdock assert that one may enter the circle at any point, and move either forwards or backwards, depending on the situation. For lean thinkers who work in product development, where the goal is to build knowledge, this model is intuitively akin to Allen Ward's LAMDA model (**L**ook, **A**sk, **M**odel, **D**iscuss, **A**ct,) in which new knowledge is to be preserved in each step and the new knowledge informs the next step to be taken.

In the thinking skills model of CPS, the data and knowledge gained as you move through the rhythm of divergent and convergent thinking are used to inform the executive function of "assessing the situation." As you learn more about the situation, you must make decisions about what is the right step to take to continue to solve the problem. Perhaps you need to go back and gather more data, or you need to develop additional options for your solution. Constantly assessing the situation means that you do not blindly move forward through the process if the knowledge you have gained indicates you need to repeat or advance a step or move back to a previous step. From a lean thinking perspective, especially in product development, we know that when a PDCA cycle is run that the purpose of the "check" (or "study") step is to ensure that we decide on our next action based on what we have learned, and not on what a previously created plan or process might say.

I'm not suggesting you give up lean thinking for CPS! Far from it. But do you think there might be situations when following a CPS process is helpful?

Notes

1. www.creativeeducationfoundation.org/creative-problem-solving/the-cps-process/.
2. Puccio, G. J., Mance, M., and Murdock, M. C. *Creative Leadership: Skills that Drive Change* (London: SAGE, 2011).

Appendix 5

A3s and CPS

An A3 is essentially a storyboard for solving a problem. Each step of the problem-solving process is documented on a large piece of paper (ledger size in the US, A3 in the rest of the world). The A3 is a tool to not only solve a problem, but also to make the thinking of the problem-solver visible, and so it is ideal for a manager to understand their employee's thinking approach, and coach them to "think more deeply." If you're not familiar with A3 problem-solving, John Shook's *Managing to Learn*, gives a brilliant description of both the problem-solving and the coaching process.

Not all problems require an A3, and some problems are too thorny for a single A3. A3s are living documents – the first version of an A3 will look very different from the final version, because the A3 process drives learning and deeper understanding, which results in many updates to everything from the title, to the goals, to the planned countermeasures.

How might creative thinking be used with an A3? The divergent thinking/convergent thinking heartbeat of creative thinking fits well with the A3, because:

- the A3 is built on the PDCA cycle;
- the A3 format requires effective convergent thinking in order to provide succinct and clear summaries in every section;
- the A3 demands deep thinking – which is creative thinking.

At its simplest level, there are opportunities for divergent and convergent thinking and using CPS tools in nearly every section of an A3. Let's look.

Every A3 looks different – there are no "required" sections of an A3, so the examples in this book are just that, examples. But all A3s

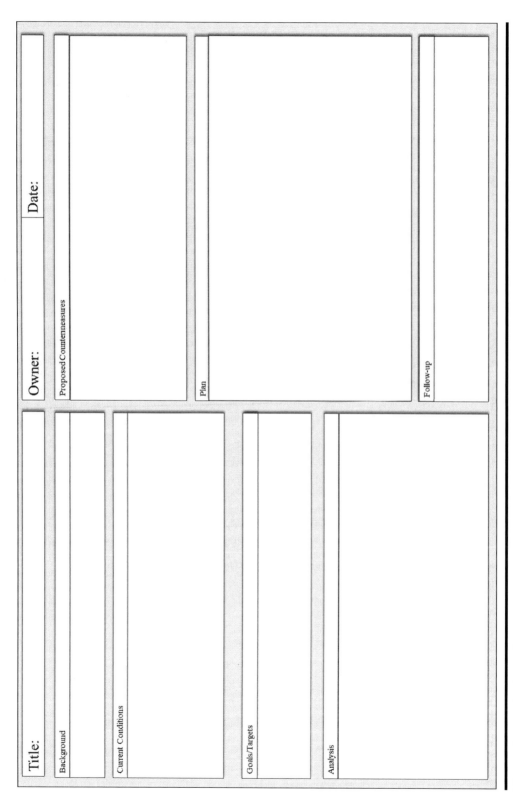

Figure A5.1 A3 Template.

start by describing the problem to be solved and end not only with countermeasures to the problem but also with a good summary of what should happen next.

In our example, the A3 has the following sections:

- Title
- Name of owner
- Date and version number
- Background
- Current conditions
- Goals/Targets
- Analysis
- Proposed countermeasures
- Plan
- Follow-up

Title

The title describes the problem to be solved. Remember when Beth was trying to decide what problem she wanted to focus her PDCA cycle on? She had to use both divergent and convergent thinking to discern the problem and narrow it down. People who use A3s will tell you that the title they start with is rarely the title they end with. As they work through the A3, they see the problem through different perspectives and update the title of their A3. But why not start with acknowledging that the initial impression of the problem is probably inaccurate? Spending time, especially with colleagues, to clarify the problem, is a beneficial way to initiate the A3, and start to build buy-in for the eventual countermeasures. This is an opportunity to use CPS tools.

Owner

The person who is the owner of the A3 is responsible for learning what needs to be learned for the problem to be solved. This doesn't mean that they do it on their own. The A3 owner must get input from others. They can do this by going to see what is going on (going to the *gemba*), by interviewing people, and by sharing their A3 in progress. Each of these activities is an opportunity to ask for more ideas and to engage others in deliberate convergent thinking. The owner always has an A3 coach, often their manager, who can encourage them to follow the rhythm of creative thinking as they coach them to think deeply at each step.

Background

This section of the A3 is used to describe how the problem came to attention. This might include a new business strategy that requires a change, or an incident that needs attention. The owner needs to decide what are the most important points to include in the background. She/he can use a deliberate convergent thinking approach to identify the factor that will be most meaningful to understanding the problem.

Current Conditions

This is a place to document data known about the problem. This might be measurements that are currently available, or the result of a data-gathering exercise like the "Five Whys" interview Beth and her team conducted. A full cycle of divergent and convergent thinking may be required to identify data related to the problem and to select the key data to include on the A3.

Goals/Targets

Goals may be provided by the organization, or they may need to be developed specifically for this problem. The use of CPS approaches can be very valuable in goal setting – to create a vision of the future, and to decide which key data will let you know you have solved the problem. In the divergent stage, the owner can brainstorm (alone or with colleagues) to generate goal statements. Starting each goal statement with a stem like "It would be great if" is very helpful. Ignore the temptation to be too practical, too soon. This is a time to think about what has never been done before, what could be done if money were no object, what should be done to ensure that the organization succeeds or that employees are fully engaged.

Title: Use CPS to clarify the problem statement	Owner:	Date:

Background

Divergent thinking: How did the problem come to our attention? What is the story of the problem?

Convergent thinking: Which parts of the story are most helpful to document?

Current Conditions

Divergent thinking: What is everything we know and can measure about the current conditions?

Convergent thinking: Which current conditions are most helpful to document?

Goals/Targets

Divergent thinking: Brainstorm on: It would be great if....

Convergent thinking: Which of these attributes best reflect the state when the problem is solved?

Divergent thinking: How might we measure these attributes of the future state?

Convergent thinking: Which attributes provide a sufficient, balanced set of measures?

Analysis

Divergent thinking: What are all potential root causes?

Convergent thinking: Which of these root causes are the most important to address?

Divergent thinking: What are all the ways we could test the validity of our root cause hypothesis?

Convergent thinking: Which test will give us the best, fastest confirmation for the least cost?

Proposed Countermeasures

Divergent thinking: What are all the potential countermeasures?

Convergent thinking: Which of these countermeasures have the best chance of success?

Divergent thinking: What are all the ways we could test our countermeasures?

Convergent thinking: Which test will give us the best, fastest confirmation for the least cost?

Plan

Divergent thinking: What are all the potential barriers to implementation?

Convergent thinking: Which of these barriers should we address first? What actions should we take?

Divergent thinking: What are all the ways we could pilot our implementation plan?

Convergent thinking: Which actions must we take first?

Follow-up

Divergent thinking: What is everything we learned in solving this problem?

Convergent thinking: Which learnings are the most valuable to document and share?

Figure A5.2 Creative Problem Solving A3.

Convergent thinking, using tools like clustering, dot voting, and finally formulating the goals into "SMART" (**S**pecific, **M**easurable, **A**ttainable, **R**elevant and **T**ime-Based) goals, closes the creative thinking cycle in this stage. Take the "A" in SMART with a grain of salt. There are times when a goal that is not apparently "attainable" is necessary, especially when safety is involved. For more on this, explore the story of the transformation at Alcoa, led by Paul O'Neill.

Analysis

In this section, the owner documents the results of their investigation into the problem. There are many lean tools to use in analysis – for example, the fishbone diagram, "the Five Whys," value stream mapping, Pareto charts. Remember that the rhythm of creativity continues during analysis. CPS tools and approaches enrich the use of the lean tools. For example, the owner of the A3 could lead a brainstorm session on factors to be included in a draft fishbone diagram. Convergent thinking can aid the owner in selecting which factors to explore first. As the owner and colleagues explore the factors and come to understand their relationship, key factors will stand out as potentially being the root causes of the problem. Validating these factors will require testing – and again, the owner must use divergent thinking (what are all the potential ways to test this?) and convergent thinking (which is the best, fastest test that will get me the data I need?) to move forward. Of course, these are PDCA cycles!

Proposed Countermeasures

Countermeasures are the changes that the owner will recommend to solve the problem. A complex problem often will require more than one countermeasure. It may be that there are known and tested solutions for the problem the owner is working on. But if the problem is complex or new, she/he is going to need to seek innovative countermeasures, and that will require deep, creative thinking.

It is very important to recognize that the owner may not be the person who comes up with the ideas that eventually solve the problem. The owner of the A3 has the responsibility to find the countermeasures – but they may come from many potential sources. A well-prepared A3 is an excellent way to bring colleagues and stakeholders up to speed on the problem, its history, and the results of the owner's analysis. The owner can review the A3 with colleagues, and then facilitate a brainstorming session to identify potential countermeasures.

Once the group comes up with a good set of ideas, they can use convergent thinking and tools to select the countermeasures to test. As in the Analysis section, selecting and planning tests may require their own creative cycle.

Plan

Although the "Plan" section is often used through the life of the A3 to document the steps the owner will take, this section is most critical when the owner is planning to implement the new countermeasures. It is common knowledge that most projects fail in the implementation stage. Despite every effort the owner has made to include others in the process, it is often unlikely that every person impacted by recommended changes will have been involved or will agree with and support the changes. In one sense, this is a new problem for the owner to solve. Indeed, if making the change is not treated as a problem to solve, the owner may find that understanding the factors that will assist and resist the implementation, working on getting others on board, and finally getting to the goal state may be more challenging than "solving" the problem. When preparing for implementation, there are many opportunities to think deeply by using divergent and convergent thinking.

Follow-up

The owner uses this section to describe what should happen next. How will the changes be maintained? What might be the next improvements? What key learnings from solving this problem need to become part of organizational documentation? Deciding what are the key topics to include in the follow-up section is a convergent thinking activity. A well-composed follow-up section is a gift to the organization, because it encapsulates the powerful learning accomplished during the A3 process.

PRACTICE THIS TODAY

If you're using A3s, identify where in your A3 you could have used wider divergent thinking to ensure you considered a more impactful range of options. Where could you have used stronger convergent thinking to drive focus and simplicity, and strengthen your options?

Reference

Shook, J. (2009) *Managing to Learn: Using the A3 Management Process to Solve Problems, Gain Agreement, Mentor, and Lead.* Cambridge, MA: The Lean Enterprise Institute.

Appendix 6

Discussion Questions for Self-Study or Book Club Use

1. At the beginning of the story, Linda and Carlo needed to work out how to align their philosophies, tools, and methodologies. Were you surprised that they could work together? Where do you see the opportunities for alignment and where do you see challenges in aligning lean thinking and creative thinking? Where do you see conflicts among improvement methodologies? What drives those conflicts? What could be done to learn from other approaches? Do you have a preferred system for improvement? What are your reasons for incorporating (or not incorporating) other approaches?

2. At the beginning of the book, Beth is mired in emails and meetings. Is this work? Is this the work a manager needs to do? If you're in this state, why do you think it is happening? What are the root causes? Are they systemic or personal? Contrast Beth's workday at the end of the book. Do you believe this is realistic? What did Beth need to commit to in order to work in this way? What needed to change at GPS?

3. Beth, Roberta, Keisha, and Mo all experience growth and change during the story. What do you see as the drivers of that change? What did each person need to give up? What did they need to start doing? Compare their journeys with yours. What have you given up (or will you give up) to become a lean leader? What did you or will you commit to?

4. Throughout the story, Carlo stresses the need to use both divergent and convergent thinking. When is it necessary to use divergent thinking and convergent thinking to "think deeper?" What benefits do you see to looking for opportunities to seek a wider range of options and ideas as you solve problems? When is it not prudent to do so? Why is it important to follow the guidelines for divergent thinking and convergent thinking?

5. All tools for divergent thinking are variations of brainstorming, but convergent thinking tools come in many varieties. Why do you think that is? What are the purposes of tools for convergent thinking? What convergent thinking tools do you use now?

6. It does you no good to come up with a great idea, if you can't get it accepted. What tools for gaining acceptance did you see in the story? What is the difference between gaining consensus and gaining acceptance?

7. Creativity is more than using tools. What might you do to build your creativity? How do you or might you feed your mind with ideas from different fields of study, art, music, and physical movement? How do you or might you allow your subconscious to create connections and "bake" ideas? What is the value of non-work activities, such as playing an instrument, participating in sports, singing in a choir, practicing yoga, walking outside, meditating?

8. Where else do you think Beth might use what she has learned outside of her professional life?

9. What ideas from this book are you planning to adopt? Where are you curious to learn more?

Resources: Books and Websites for Further Learning

On Creative Problem Solving

Books

Miller, B., Vehar, J., Firestien, R., Thurber, S., and Neilsen, D. (2011) *Creativity Unbound: An Introduction to Creative Process*, 5th edn. Scituate, MA: FourSight, LLC.

Puccio, G. J., Mance, M., and Murdock, M. C. (2911) *Creative Leadership: Skills that Drive Change*. London: SAGE.

Websites

International Center for Studies in Creativity (SUNY Buffalo State): https://creativity.buffalostate.edu/.

The Creative Education Foundation: www.creativeeducationfoundation.org/

The Creative Problem Solving Institute Conference: http://cpsiconference.com/

On Lean Thinking

Books

These are a handful of the books that Linda recommended to Beth.

Ballé M. and Ballé, F. (2014) *Lead with Respect: A Novel of Lean Practice*. Cambridge, MA: The Lean Enterprise Institute.

Morgan, J. M. and Liker, J. K. (2019) *Designing the Future: How Ford, Toyota, and Other World-Class Organizations Use Lean Product Development to Drive Innovation and Transform Their Business*. New York: McGraw-Hill.

Ross, K. (2019) *How to Coach for Creativity in Service Excellence: A Lean Coaching Workbook*. London: Routledge/Productivity Press.

Rother, M. (2010) *Toyota Kata: Managing People for Improvement, Adaptiveness and Superior Results.* New York: McGraw-Hill.

Shook, J. (2009) *Managing to Learn: Using the A3 Management Process to Solve Problems, Gain Agreement, Mentor, and Lead.* Cambridge, MA: The Lean Enterprise Institute.

Websites

Kata to Grow (Kata in the Classroom): www.katatogrow.com/
The Lean Enterprise Institute: www.lean.org
The Lean Product and Process Development Exchange: www.lppde.org

On Lean Thinking and Creative Problem Solving

Website

www.leanforhumans.com

Index

Please note: page numbers in *italic type* indicate figures/illustrations